HANDWRITING
&
PALMISTRY

HANDWRITING
&
PALMISTRY

Discover Personality and Potential from Handwriting and Hands

Liz Gerstein

Nouvelle Press
Potomac, Maryland

Additional copies of this book may be ordered through bookstores
or by sending $17.95 plus $3.50 for postage and handling to:
Publishers Distribution Service
6893 Sullivan Road
Grawn, MI 49637
(800) 345-0096

Publisher's Cataloging-in-Publication Data

Gerstein, Liz, —
    Handwriting & Palmistry : discover personality and
    potential from handwriting and hands / by Liz
    Gerstein—Potomac, Maryland : Nouvelle Press.
        p.   ill.   cm.
    Includes bibliographical references and index.
    ISBN: 0-9636319-0-X
    1. Graphology. 2. Palmistry. I. Title.
    BF891.G   1993
    155.282—dc20   93-83828

Manufactured in the United States of America.

10 9 8 7 6 5 4 3 2 1

Book Design by Alex Moore / PDS

IN APPRECIATION FOR THE MORAL SUPPORT

OF MY FRIENDS AND FAMILY

Preface

As a professional and nationally certified handwriting analyst, I have also become deeply immersed in "scientific palmistry." From the beginning of my studies, a strong interplay of correlating features began to emerge between the hands and the handwriting.

Is it not amazing and fascinating that each person in this universe has his inimitable fingerprints, so unique that they serve as a means of identification? And there are no two handwritings exactly alike, even though they may strongly resemble each other, there are a host of variances present. In fact, more than 2000 separate traits and symbols can be isolated, although not in any one individual's handwriting alone. —Compounding this diversity with those indicators seen in the hands, palms and fingers, the combinations are infinite, which makes each person's hands and handwriting special.

The physical aspect of the hand is called "chirognomy," derived from the Greek word "kheir," meaning "hand," and "chirognomy," the study of the hands. These are, as is our general physical makeup, largely governed by our genetic code. The hands may carry, along with signs of talent, innate abilities as well as some unfavorable tendencies and predispositions toward diseases. To be made aware of these can be beneficial; by using proper diets and physical fitness, these negative tendencies may remain dormant forever.

I don't want to be known as "Gypsy-Liz," the fortune or future-teller. The length of a person's life, impending success or disasters, should not and cannot be accurately predicted. Such practices of sensationalism should be avoided by an analyst. My aim in evaluating hands and handwriting is to guide people, to emphasize their potential in professional and personal areas, and, if necessary, to help them with their shortcomings, which we all have.

The handwriting mirrors our mental, emotional and physical health and well-being at the time of writing. Everyone recognizes the fact that it can fluctuate from day to day, and sometimes from moment to moment, which is confirmation that our hand is only the tool of the brain impulses, just as the brain's impulses have etched the lines and intricate patterns into our hands and fingers.

I am writing this to foster an interest and awareness of our hands and handwriting, and the exciting facts they reveal. They provide pieces of the very complex puzzle that is our SELF.

Contents

Introduction

GENERAL PRINCIPLES AND HISTORIES
OF PALMISTRY AND GRAPHOLOGY

MY AIM IN WRITING THIS BOOK WAS TO INTRODUCE THE STUDIES OF THE HANDS and handwriting in the hope of wetting your appetite, so that many of you will want to immerse yourselves deeper into these subjects and their fascinating inter-relation.

That the hands and handwriting should have a common thread is not a far-fetched idea because as each part of our physical and mental/emotional make-up is a piece of our personality, each of us is linked to a culture and to mankind.

All through the ages - from the Egyptians, Greeks, Romans and Chinese, to the present - scientists and scholars, as well as charlatans and "sidewalk prophets," have attempted to predict the future with crystal balls, star gazing, astrology, and the reading of the cards, hands and handwriting. Yet the theory that a person's fate is sealed from the "cradle to the grave," or even from the moment of conception, has been proved wrong, because our fate or destiny is largely of our own making and we have a strong role in shaping it. The individual who is aware of the strengths and weaknesses within himself and wants to find out "what makes him tick" has the greatest chances of self-directing his destiny. Those who prefer to "play ostrich" by closing their eyes to their own shortcomings gain little awareness of themselves and others, and usually blame circumstances and bad luck for their misfortunes.

Learning to look at hands and handwriting with understanding and honesty will give a person additional insight into his personality. In this book, I am trying to show that no trait or symbol should ever be interpreted on its own merit. This pertains to Chirognomy/Palmistry, as well as to Graphology. Only when the hand and writing are examined holistically will they show a strong interrelation.

Examination reveals that the lines in the hands are not caused by flexing or folding of the fingers and palm. Rather, they are etched into the palm as a result of thought processes by our master computer, the brain. An infant is born with its own blueprint of inherent characteristics, some of which are reflected in the shape and structure of the hands, in the lines and other markings imprinted on the palmar surface, the fingers and thumb prints. These are established in the fetus around the eighteenth week of pregnancy, and are the result of impulses received from the central nervous system.

Some hands have very few lines engraved on them. This is not caused by a lack of manual work; often the opposite is the case. A farmer or someone who works primarily with his hands may have fewer lines than the individual whose main activity is mental rather than physical. The lines are a reflection of our central nervous system. Few but strong major lines - those of Life, Heart and Head - indicate a calm disposition, and are a reflection of firmly rooted practical goals. A palm covered with a network of spiderweb-like lines reveals a highly sensitive and often over-excitable nervous system. Lines, especially the "secondary lines," are subject to alterations as they register changes in a person's desires and attitudes, and in his mental and physical health.

Just as the lines on the palmar surface are subject to modification, so is a person's handwriting. One of the questions I am asked constantly is why writing changes when someone is in a hurry or depressed. Some people mention that they have different styles of writing when they write to friends and family, versus business. Many use printscript for professional communication and a cursive style when writing personal letters. Although these variations are usually chosen subconsciously, the individual is aware of them but cannot explain them. The answer to these questions is identical to the one pertaining to the lines and creases on the palm, namely, that the handwriting is also governed by the impulses and thought processes of our mastermind, the brain; thus, it is not surprising that these sciences should be interrelated.

Our hand is merely a tool that guides the pen in more or less rhythmic movements, and exacts more or less pressure on the writing surface. The rhythm of writing is a subconscious and automatic reflection of our functioning, and the pressure reveals our intensity of will and vitality, which are explained in PART III- Chapters 20 and 23.

If the hand is not able to guide the pen, as is the case when injured or absent, a person may train himself to grip the pen with his toes or teeth, which produces the same characteristics pertaining to his character and personality. If the writing appears tremulous, the handwriting analyst will suspect a handicap in one area or another. Where a physical handicap is ruled out, a tremor may be caused by a physiological disorder such as Parkinson's disease, or it can be the result of emotional or psychological conflicts such as extreme internal pressure or agitation.

Helen Keller is an outstanding example of a person who conquered severe physical handicaps caused by an inflammation of the brain, usually present in encephalitis, that destroyed her sight and hearing before she was two years old. Because of this condition, she was unable to speak, and was entirely shut off from the world until her father took her to Dr. Alexander Graham Bell, who advised him to write to the Perkins Institute for the Blind, in Boston. Shortly before Helen was seven years old, Anne Sullivan arrived from Boston to teach her to write, working out an alphabet by spelling words on Helen's hand. Later, the child was able to connect words with objects. Helen also learned to speak, although until the age of ten she could only talk with the sign language of the deaf-mute. Her printscript handwriting still reflected her superior intelligence and vitality in spite of her many handicaps.

THE HISTORY OF PALMISTRY

The origins of palmistry may be much older than previously surmised. Some anthropologists believe that the handprints found in prehistoric caves date back to the Stone Age, and were used in religious initiation ceremonies.

We do know that hand reading was well known in Greece from the fourth Century B.C. on, when the reign of Alexander the Great had made its progression from Northern India. It is said that Alexander, who was brave and fearless in battles, also showed concern and interest about his future by delving into all methods of prophesy, including astrology, graphology and hand reading. Aristotle, the philosopher who was also Alexander's tutor, imparted much knowledge of this science to him and other students. According to Elizabeth Daniels Squire's book, "Palmistry Made Practical," Aristotle's manuscript on general physiognomy included information on the shape, color and texture of the hands.

It is only fitting that the study of the hands should be called "Chirognomy," which is derived from the Greek word "Kheir" meaning "hand" and "Chiromantia/Chiromancy," which was the name given to the study of the linear surface and patterns of the palm. This was later popularized by "Palmistry," which is derived from the Latin roots "Paume," meaning "palm." This reveals that even in those days the studies of the hand and of the palmar surface were divided into different sciences, with chirognomy relating to the outer structure, skin texture and all physical aspects of the hand, and palmistry encompassing the linear patterns of the palm, fingers and thumb tips that serve as a never-changing means of identification. These grooves are referred to as "papillary ridges" and are divided into four basic patterns; i.e., the Arch, Tented Arch, Loop and Whorl, which will be discussed in PART II, Chapter 11 of this book.

In modern times, the medical team of Drs. Ruth Achs and Rita Harper used dermatoglyphics, as the study of these papillary ridges is called, to find hard-to-detect birth defects in babies whose mothers had German measles during pregnancy. This research was implemented in a Brooklyn, New York, hospital in the 1950's.

The oldest known manuscript on palmistry in the English language is the "Digby Roll IV," which is in the Bodleian Library in Oxford, England. It is called "Summa Chiromantia," and was printed before 1440 A.D. Another manuscript from that era exists in the library of Princeton University, Princeton, New Jersey.

That people were interested in the study of the hands during the Renaissance is clearly portrayed by painters such as Albrecht Duerer of Germany, whose famous painting of the "Praying Hands" depicts in detail the Intuitive/Sensitive type of hand, which is characterized by a long, narrow palm and long fingers. (PART I, Chapter 1 in this book). In his self-portrait as a young man, Duerer painted his hands with a very prominent, bulbous thumb, a feature which was later referred to as the "murderer's thumb," giving evidence of a quick and explosive temper, a trait Duerer was known to possess.

The 16th and 17th Centuries brought forth a number of prominent scientists who advanced the science of palmistry. Among them was Baron John von Haagen, better known as John Indagine the Friar, who wrote "Introductus Apoletesmaticae." Another scholar was Taisnier, whose writings were published in 1562. One notable German scientist and medical doctor was Heinrich Lutz, who wrote "La Chiromancia Medicinale" and "Cheirosophia Concentrata," concentrating his research and studies on medicine. Another outstanding luminary in this field was Johannes Praetorius, born in 1630, whose writings were included in the official curriculum of the University of Leipzig, Germany.

When gypsies from Northern India swarmed over Europe, they brought with them a different kind of palmistry. Their aura of mysticism contributed to the fear and fascination people had for their predictions. Sadly, their prophecies often materialized through the power of positive or negative suggestion, which only strengthened people's fears and belief in the Gypsies' fortune - and misfortune-telling abilities.

The Gypsies found their way to the court of England. It was rumored that King Henry VIII was a staunch believer of palmistry. The portraits of him clearly accentuate his hands, which were prominently displayed with rings on his index and little fingers. Rings worn on the index finger, especially on the right hand, allow no doubts as to a person's desire and quest for power, while rings worn on the little fingers by men suggest some peculiarity or difficulties with regard to intimate relationships, generally relating back to early parental relationships.

Among the luminaries of the 18th Century was Capt. Stanislas d'Arpigny of France, (1798-1865), who received his first knowledge of palmistry from a gypsy. Obviously fascinated, he went on to study the old masters such as Taisnier and Indagine. He then developed his own ideas and techniques, one of which is the classification of six basic hand types and one "mixed type," still being used today. Because of this new technique, he is considered by many to be the father of modern palmistry, a fame that is shared or disputed by followers of Adolphe Desbarolles of France, (1801-1886).

Probably the most colorful and charismatic palm reader, author and lecturer was Count Louis Hamon, (1866-1936), better known by his "nom de guerre" Cheiro, meaning "hand reader." "Language Of The Hand," one of his first books, gained immense recognition and was first printed in 1897, in England. It was subsequently reprinted thirty-three times in that country and in the United States, even though Cheiro died in 1936. Another well known book was his "Palmistry For All," published in 1915, and "Cheiro's Complete Palmistry," which was published posthumously in 1968.

Cheiro was the son of a count and was sought out by royal circles and by celebrities from all over the world, including Mark Twain, Douglas Fairbanks, Erich von Strohheim and Oscar Wilde. With regards to the latter, in his book "Complete Palmistry," Cheiro recounts an anecdote, which took place during one of his fashionable parlor games, where he would analyze hands extended to him through a curtain without his knowing the owner's identity. When Oscar Wilde's hands appeared through the curtain, Cheiro exclaimed in astonishment, "the left hand is that of a king, but the right one that of a king who will send himself into exile." Wilde left without saying a word. Although the latter was the toast of London, having just produced his play "A Woman Of No Importance," he had been leading a decadent life of debauchery of which few people were aware. This was made public during the sensational trial at "Old Bailey" where Wilde was accused and convicted of sexual perversion and corruption. He was sent to prison and later into exile in France, where he died alone and shunned by his former friends. Cheiro saw in Oscar Wilde's left hand-his birth hand - brilliance and success, for this man was endowed with one of the greatest intellects and talents, but his right hand - he was right handed - revealed a negative side to Wilde's character that included self-indulgence and a propensity towards outer stimuli, which led to his downfall. Unfortunately, Cheiro does not reveal the signs and markings upon which he based his analysis, but in this book I will pinpoint some of the clusters and combinations of characteristics that could result in adversity, especially if found in the dominant hand of an individual.

Other notable palmists were Victorian scholar Heron-Allen, whose book, "A Manual Of Chirosophy," was published in 1885, and William G. Benham's "The Laws Of Scientific Hand Reading," which appeared in London and New York in 1900. Benham also received his first teachings from a gypsy, who inspired him to develop his own techniques.

The 20th Century produced, and continues to bring forth, modern scientists who advance our knowledge of chirognomy and chiromancy. Julius Spier of Switzerland focused his studies on children's hands. His book, "The Hands Of Children," was published in 1944 after Spier's untimely death. Carl G. Jung, the pioneer psychologist, wrote in the preface of Spier's book, "I have had several opportunities of observing Dr. Julius Spier at work, and must admit that the results he has achieved have made a lasting impression on me."

Noel Jaquin of Great Britain was another notable scholar who made great strides in the practical application and development of palmistry. His book, "Scientific Palmistry," was published in London in the early 1900's. His ideas were far-reaching when he wrote that "The main object of the study of the hand is prevention," meaning the prevention of the development of latent diseases, and "the prevention of the waste of years of effort and energy spent following a career for which the individual is unfitted," thus pointing to his original studies in the field of career selection.

Among the many modern writers of palmistry is Fred Gettings, whose two books, "The Book Of The Hand," and "Palmistry," were published in 1965 and 1966 respectively. Gettings' books are not only excellent summaries of the past and present theories but of their modification and development. David Brandon-Jones' "Practical Palmistry" was published in London and the United States in 1986, and is a recent and worthwhile addition of scientific palmistry. He sees this science as a key to self-knowledge and character analysis.

There is a vast difference between the palmistry of 500 years ago and that of today. The main change is the realization that no sign or symbol seen in the hands should be isolated and interpreted on its own merit. All findings must be cross-checked against other factors to form a "Gestalt." Only when taken seriously and scientifically can hand reading become a tool for vocational guidance, selection of marriage partners or compatibility; it could also be a valuable adjunct to medical research, as exemplified earlier with regards to newborns whose mothers contracted German measles during pregnancy.

William Benham and Noel Jaquin were pioneers in predicting that some of palmistry's greatest and most valuable applications would be in the area of vocational guidance and marriage counseling.

Not much emphasis is made by today's palmists on predicting the future, because it is recognized that the lines in the hands are subject to changes and alterations both favorably and unfavorably. This is referred to as evolution or integration and involution or disintegration. It is my opinion that one of the most valuable aspects of palmistry is the insight and self-awareness gained from the study of the hands, which in turn can lead to self-improvement, adjustment and happiness. And, I might add, the exploration into what is written in our hands is a truly fascinating experience.

THE HISTORY OF GRAPHOLOGY

During the Renaissance, many people became aware of the difference in graphic expression from one person to another. The first attempt to interpret handwriting systematically and to categorize the individual characteristics and symbols was made by Dr. Camillo Baldi, a professor at the University of Bologna, Italy. Baldi's manuscript, published in 1625, translates into "how to recognize the nature and quality of a writer from his letters." His teachings were included in the university's curriculum. Sadly, this science lapsed into obscurity after Baldi's death.

In the early 19th Century, the French Abbot Jean-Hypolite Michon, (1806-1881) coined the word "graphology," translated literally as "the science of writing." His work, "Systeme De Graphologie," was published in 1875, and consists of a systematic tabulation of graphic signs and symbols in writing as they relate to the study of character. Michon's disciple, J. Crepieux-Jamin, (1858-1940), continued his professor's work and adding to it his own research resulted in "L'Ecriture Et Le Caractere," (The Handwriting and Character).

Notable students of graphology of that period included Sir Walter Scott, British Statesman Benjamin Disraeli, and British poet Robert Browning.

In 1836, author R.I. Stevenson's ground-breaking book, "The Strange Case Of Dr. Jekyll and Mr. Hyde," dealt with his subject's schizophrenic phases of pleasantness and choleric nastiness. Stevenson showed his interest in graphology clearly by comparing Hyde's writing with that of Dr. Jekyll, remarking on the resemblance and the dissimilarities of the two writings.

At the beginning of the 20th Century, many European scientists began to show renewed interest in the development of graphology. Dr. Ludwig Klages, a German philosopher and psychologist, decided to make this science his life's work. He is considered the "father of modern graphology" because of his theory that the writing must be interpreted holistically as a "Gestalt," and not merely from a compilation of fragmented signs or symbols. Although his famous book "Handschrift Und Character," was in its 23rd printing in 1949, in Germany, no attempt has been made to translate it into English. Strange as it seems, the United States has been unreceptive toward this science until recent years, and all books on that subject were classified in the occult section of libraries and book stores, lumped together with books on witchcraft.

As a psychologist, Dr. Klages realized that understanding of basic principles of psychology must be a prerequisite to becoming a handwriting analyst. Consequently, European graphologists receive very professional training.

Many other scientists followed in Dr. Klages' footsteps in recognizing that a person's handwriting is, in actuality, governed by the brain, and serves as a written expression of his emotional, physical and psychological make-up, reflecting his emotional state at the moment of writing. Among the giant proponents of this advanced theory were:

- Dr. Max Pulver, a Swiss psychologist, professor at the University of Zurich, who based his studies of handwriting on Carl Jung's depth psychology, who asserted that expression in handwriting is founded on symbolism resulting from "archetypes" which are hidden in the human soul. Pulver advanced this ground-breaking theory of the three zones in writing, i.e., the upper, middle and lower zones, which are discussed in this book in PART III, Chapter 13.

Pulver's famous book, "Symbolik Der Handschrift," (Symbolism in Handwriting), was published in 1930 and is still widely read in Europe, although not available in English translation.

- Dr. Klara Roman, who brought her knowledge of handwriting analysis from her native Hungary to the United States, taught at the New School for Social Research in California. Her book, "A Key To Personality," was published in 1952, and is still a much-used source of study and reference. Roman developed and patented a graphic device called the "Psychogram" and "Measuring Guide," which permits the analyst to extract and categorize the various characteristics from the handwriting, pertaining to the size, width, pressure, etc., and to determine from them the different modes of functioning, the ego development and social attitudes such as the extroversion and introversion of an individual.

- Dr. Robert Saudek. Born in Austria, Dr. Saudek spent his adult life in England and the United States, where he concentrated his studies of graphology on the "speed" and the "formation and pressure in strokes," which resulted in his 1928 published book, "Experiments With Handwriting."

- Dr. Werner Wolff. A professor of psychology at Bard College; his important published book, "Diagrams Of The Unconscious," was the result of his research and clinical experiments showing the impact of our subconscious mind on handwriting.

All of the above and many other scientists began to recognize the significant contribution of graphology in such fields as psychiatry, aptitudes for career choices, personnel selection and for personal or interpersonal relationships. Its potential has not yet been fully realized and harnessed.

NATIONAL CHARACTERISTICS

Just as every nation has its own "special flavor," handwriting is also influenced by nationality. English writing, for instance, is recognized by a predominantly vertical position or slant, discussed in PART III - Chapter 15, revealing the British people's natural inclination toward reserve and poise. Many capital letters show a Greek or Roman influence, which indicates a propensity for old traditions, another characteristic recognized in many British individuals.

The handwriting of people from the Latin countries, in southern Europe and South America, is generally adorned with flourishes and curves. This is a reflection of spontaneous and vivacious physical gestures - also mirrored in a colorful taste in clothing and home furnishings as well.

Because America is a melting pot of many nationalities and cultures, American handwriting reflects a pioneering and enterprising type of personality. This is a simplified script that is often stripped of non-essential strokes and void of flourishes. This kind of writing has a tendency to lean to the right, indicating a fast, forward-moving tempo. (PART III - Chapters 14 and 15 of this book).

I could go on and on about national characteristics. Ideally, the graphologist should be able to compare the method by which the individual was taught with his current writing in order to assess the changes that have occurred.

WHAT HANDWRITING DOES NOT REVEAL

Handwriting does not indicate the sex of the writer because we all carry masculine and feminine components, called animus and anima, in our genes. These are the male hormones in females and female hormones in males. As the gap has narrowed between men's and women's career opportunities, so has the handwriting become more androgynous. It is interesting to note that socio-economic changes have made an impact on handwriting.

The age of the writer is even harder to pinpoint because the handwriting measures emotional, not chronological, maturity. Many a teenager's writing displays emotional maturity beyond his years, independence of thought and decision-making, while these qualities may be lacking in senior adults.

CONCLUSIONS

I am not asking you to believe the theories and hypotheses described in this book. I urge you to find out for yourself, especially with regard to the interrelation of Chirognomy/Palmistry and Graphology. I did. I brought my interest and basic knowledge of graphology from my native Switzerland, and have been a handwriting analyst for many years in this country. While I have always had a "passing fancy" for palmistry, my interest deepened into fascination after reading the first "scientific" book I had ever come across, which was the "Book Of The Hand" by Fred Gettings, published in 1965. By checking its findings and revelations in my own hands, and those of family and friends, I began to realize the interplay and correlation of what is gleaned from the hands and what is expressed in the writing.

It is my belief that there is a "natural progression" from the left, or "birth" hand, which shows our inborn tendencies, to the right, or "dominant" hand, (in right-handed people, and vice versa if left-handed). The right hand then reveals the changes that may have taken place, discussed in PART II - Chapter 10, RIGHT HAND VERSUS LEFT HAND.

I encourage you to read this book with pencil and paper by your side. Record the findings of as many hands and handwritings as you can to build up a personal file. I promise that you will find the time spent worthwhile and fascinating.

PART ONE

―――――――

Chirognomy

☆

All physiognomical aspects of the hand, fingers and
thumb; skin texture; the Mounts or elevations.

1

The Basic Hand Types

WHEN YOU BECOME AWARE OF "HANDS," YOU WILL BEGIN TO LOOK AT THEM differently. Up until now, you probably evaluated hands merely in terms of their physical beauty or lack of it, lamenting that your nails were brittle, or that you had ugly "knuckle fingers." Now you will learn things from your own hands and from those of total strangers that you never realized or observed before.

First, your two hands may or may not be exactly alike. Close scrutiny could reveal that one finger of one hand is slightly different in size or shape, or it might bend in one hand and not in the other. The meaning of this will be further explained in PART I - Chapter 3, when discussing the fingers.

If you are right-handed, your left hand is your "birth" hand, where genetic tendencies and predispositions have left their mark, while your right hand becomes your dominant one. The reverse holds true if you are left-handed, in which case your left hand is the dominant one. If both hands, including the lines engraved in the palmar surface, are identical or not greatly different, it shows that the person's life has progressed pretty well along the prescribed path, or that the individual has not made great strides toward self-expression. It is the task of the palmist to interpret the hand as an entity after having recorded all the individual signs and markings.

The hands are classified into six pure - and one mixed - types, with as many subdivisions and combinations within each group. Most of us

3

have hands that are combinations of two or more types, but one category usually emerges as dominant, except in the "mixed hand." This classification of hand types, which is still used today, was originated by Stanislas d'Arpigny of France, the 19th Century scholar and one of the luminaries in the science of palmistry.

I will begin with the most primitive hand type, which is rarely encountered in the civilized world, at least not in its pure form. Yet, there are hands that approach its shape and texture to a degree. The rest of the hand types are not classified according to "more or less" advanced personality types.

THE ELEMENTARY OR CLUMSY HAND
(Figure 1, a-d)

This hand in its pure form would have a large, coarse and thick palm, with short stubby fingers and nails. (Figure 1 a) The texture of the skin in palm and fingers would also be coarse, with heavy skin ridges. There would be few lines engraved on the palmar surface (Figure 1 b), such as the necessary Lifeline, and short or nonexistent lines of Head (mentality) and Heart (emotional capacity). The thumb would be extremely short (Figure 1 c), barely reaching the first section of the index finger when the hand is closed. This shortness of the thumb is an atavistic or regressive sign, seen in the "hands" of apes and primates. If the top section of such a thumb is especially heavy or bulbous (Figure 1 d), it gives a clue to a violent temper, which a person possessing this kind of mentality would be unable to control. Should he commit an act of aggression or murder, it would be in the fury of anger or passion and not premeditation.

The owner of such a hand would have a perfect indifference about anything except his basic needs of sex and survival. He would possess little imagination or ambition. Since this hand belongs to the "Earth" type, he would be best suited for unskilled manual labor.

In addition to the negative features of this hand, it also has innate positive characteristics, such as instinctual love and protection toward his family and animals. The bearer of such a hand possesses a fierce loyalty, but he is guided by instinct rather than by reason, much as the higher form of animals.

THE SQUARE OR USEFUL HAND
(Figure 2 a-d)

The Square hand in its pure form has a broad, square palm (Figure 2 a), with fingers set squarely in the hand (Figure 2 b). The fingers themselves are thick and square with broad fingertips (Figure 2 c). It is also likely that the fingernails are broader than long (Figure 2 d). People with this kind of hand are practical and precise in manner, less from inborn grace than from the need for conformity and habits. They respect authority and law and order. Through perseverance and the strength of a plodding will, they often bypass other more brilliant people in success and achievement. Even in the face of adversities, such people are loyal and honest in business. Their strongest fault lies in the fact that they perceive things in black and white, and understand only that which can be explained by reason and logic, which makes such individuals seem obstinate and intolerant at times. There are many subdivisions and modifications of the "pure" Square hand, which add new characteristics to the personality, yet it does not change the fact that people possessing a square palm are looking for practical, viable solutions to problems.

The Square Palm With Long Fingers:

This hand shows a greater propensity toward "theory," yet its bearer makes decisions based on logic and reason. It is not surprising that many engineers and architects have this type of hand.

The Square Palm With Knotty Fingers: (see Figure 4 c)

This hand is generally found with long fingers and well-developed joints, which show love of detail and analytical thinking. If such a hand is found among people in the medical profession or science of any kind, the love of detail will make an excellent specialist or researcher, because these individuals strive for perfection.

The Square Palm With Spatulate Fingers: (see Figure 3 a)

Fingers that are flared and widen toward the tip are referred to as "spatulate" and are often encountered in hands where the palm is also of a slightly triangular shape (see Figure 3). People possessing such spatulate fingertips belong to the "inventors;" they either improve on

standard practices or invent something new! Their inventions are
always on a practical plane, indicated by the square shape of the palm.

The Square Palm With Rounded Fingertips: (see Figure 5 b)

Fingers that are rounded or "conic" toward the tips express a combination of practical goals with an artistic bent, be it music, literature
or art. It is a favorable combination to have, because such an individual will be able to exert his skills to the greatest advantage.

The Square Palm With Psychic Fingers: (see Figure 6 b)

"Psychic fingers" are long and pointed toward the end. This combination of palm and fingers is rarely seen since it would bring opposites together, which results in a complex personality. Long, pointed
fingers and nails belong to the contemplative and passive, rather than
the action-loving person. Such people would start projects in a practical fashion, but might give in to moods of caprice. An example of this
"modus operandi" would be the artist who has a mass of unfinished
paintings in his studio.

The Square Palm With Long Fingers: (see Figure 7 b)

Generally, our fingers do not have identical tips. The index and
little fingers and often the ring finger as well, are more tapered toward
the tip than the middle finger. However, if the shapes and sizes of the
fingers and thumbs vary excessively, it is referred to as "mixed." If
accompanied by a supple thumb that is arched outward from the middle
joint, it reflects an extremely versatile personality, but the squareness
of the palm would also let its owner see the practical side of things.
For want of continuity and persistence, however, he will rarely rise to
great heights of success.

THE SPATULATE OR ENERGETIC HAND
(Figure 3, a-c)

The spatulate hand is so called not only because the fingers are
flared at the nail sections (Figure 3 a), but also because the palm
resembles a spatula, and is either wider at the wrist section (Figure 3
b) or at the base of the fingers (Figure 3 c). If the greater development

is at the wrist, the person is full of restless energy on a physical plane. His line of work should utilize this strong physical force; a desk job would be unsatisfying to him. Broader development at the base of the fingers indicates that its owner uses logic and reasoning abilities to the fullest. Either way, the nature of these people has a restless quality with a love of action. Wherever this hand is encountered, its owner is sure to put his stamp of individuality on it.

As a rule, the spatulate hand is medium to large with well-developed fingers that are wider at the top. The nails may be of varied shapes; if the nails are shorter than long, the person is likely to be impatient and critical.

One of the most striking characteristics of people with the Spatulate hand is the need for independence and individuality. They usually venture out into their own businesses or professions for which their pioneering spirit and individuality is best suited. In relationships, the owner of the Spatulate hand is usually loyal and honest, but he needs enough breathing space or he would get to resent the ties.

THE PHILOSOPHIC OR INTELLECTUAL HAND
(Figure 4, a-d)

The shape of this hand is easily recognized. It is characterized by a long, angular palm (Figure 4 a) with long bony fingers and well-developed finger joints (Figure 4 b), generally accompanied by long fingernails (Figure 4 c). Generally, the palmar surface is marked with more lines than the "major" ones of Life, Head and Heart (Figure 4 d).

These hands belong to the scholars, the deep thinkers and the poets. Bearers of such hands are lovers of details; they weigh all the pro's and con's of a situation very carefully, so much so that they often miss opportunities, having lost the right moment for action. People with these hands have a natural leaning toward law and order, especially if the finger joints are well-developed.

Long, smooth and pointed fingers indicate the reverse; these individuals reveal quick, intuitive perceptions and responses. It is small wonder that yogis, and spiritual leaders of the clergy quite often possess such long, tapered fingers.

Hands of the Philosophic/Intellectual type can be found everywhere, and among all professions. In the field of medicine, such a person would be ideally suited for research, especially if the finger joints are well-developed, indicating love of details and perfectionism. It is un-likely that he would be a general practitioner for want of bedside manners and personal warmth. This is not to say that the owner of this hand type lacks feelings, but his concern would most likely be for mankind rather than for the individual.

If the palm is very oblong in shape, it depicts a very sensitive disposition, and one somewhat removed from reality. This tendency is further accentuated if criss-crossed by a host of lines. In that case, the balance of the person's energies is unevenly distributed.

THE CONIC OR ARTISTIC HAND
(Figure 5, a-c)

This hand is usually medium-sized with a rounded palm that tapers slightly toward the base of the fingers (Figure 5 a). The fingers them-selves are generally of a smooth skin texture with cone-shaped or rounded fingertips and nails (Figure 5 b). If the fingers are full at the base section, it indicates a love of luxury and comfort (Figure 5 c).

The main characteristics of the Conic hand are spontaneity and intuition. People possessing this type of hand are quick in thought and ideas, therefore making very witty conversationalists. They grasp the meaning of a subject rapidly, but are often satisfied with a super-ficial knowledge of it. Generally, they do not become scholars, only because they like to spread themselves thinly over a large area rather than concentrate on one subject. They also have the tendency to form judgments quickly based on their hunches, which quite often prove them well, but it also makes them rely too much on first impressions of people and things. Individuals with the Conic/Artistic hand are generous by nature; they give freely, and usually on the spur of the moment. This hand is referred to as "Artistic" mostly with regard to temperament, and not as much to the actual producer of artistic ideas.

If the Conic hand is firm and elastic, it brings out the best qualities of its type. It reveals greater energy and firmness of will than the hand that is soft and puffy at the base of the fingers, and over-development of the Mounts. This will be discussed further in PART I, Chapter 6. The firm hand still possesses quickness of wit, and its owner will sparkle in company and among strangers. It is needless to say that such hands are often encountered among actors, politicians and public speakers; they belong to all people who are engaged in "emotional careers," which includes salesmanship. Such individuals possess an inborn feel for public awareness, and they respond to inspirations of the moment before they consciously use reason and logic.

The Conic Hand With Square Fingers: (see Figure 2 b)

People possessing this combination of hand types may rise to fame and fortune faster and surer than those with a Conic hand and like fingertips. This will be achieved by different means, such as by application of energy and endurance. These individuals are exact in their methods and practical in their application, and their innate staying power helps them to achieve their goals and expectations.

The Conic Hand With Spatulate Fingers: (see Figure 3 a)

This combination will put an innovative and individualistic touch on everything that the owner of these hands undertakes. The painter will add his own brand of design and color to his work, and the architect produces new buildings!

THE PSYCHIC/INTUITIVE HAND
(Figure 6, a-c)

This is the most beautiful and elegant, but also the most unfortunate hand to possess in terms of palmistry, but it is rarely seen in pure form. However, many hands approach this type to various degrees.

This type of hand is long, narrow and delicate-looking (Figure 6 a). When shaking hands with such a person, the hand feels boneless; one is instinctively afraid of crushing the bones with a firm handshake. The tapering fingers are equally long and delicate, with long, almond-shaped nails. This hand's very fineness and beauty indicates a lack of robust strength; the owner is poorly equipped for the harshness of living.

Individuals with the Psychic hand possess a purely visionary, idealistic nature. They appreciate the beautiful in every shape and form. Generally, they are gentle in manner, have a quiet disposition, and instinctively trust everyone who is kind to them, which makes them an easy prey for ruthless people. They respond to color and music, and are affected by religious ceremonies, being more impressed by them than by the spoken word of the sermon. Since the sensitive and intuitive faculties of these individuals are so highly developed, they often make excellent mediums and clairvoyants.

Parents who have children with such hands don't understand them unless they possess the same handtype. It often happens that these children are the off-spring of quite matter-of-fact people who, through their own lack of sensitivity and knowledge, try to guide their children into careers for which they are ill-suited, such as business or technical professions. If such children grow up misunderstood, they often have feelings of uselessness with resulting melancholy; they would only apply passive resistance to pressures, since they don't have the inner and outer toughness for an active/constructive rebellion.

THE MIXED HAND
(Figure 7, a-d)

This hand is the most difficult to describe and recognize, because it differs from case to case. When discussing the Square hand with mixed fingers, there still exists the square shape of the palm that dominates and dictates the main type to a large degree. The Mixed hand is so called because it cannot be classified as either of the above discussed hand types. The fingers also belong to the various types; some fall into the pointed, square, spatulate or conic category.

The Mixed hand reflects the person with a wealth of ideas, versatility and also changeability of purpose. An individual possessing such a hand may be adaptable with regard to people and circumstances, but adaptability taken to extremes makes for a wishy-washy and erratic personality. He may be a brilliant conversationalist on topics ranging from politics to "cockfighting in Spain." It is also likely that such a person plays one or several instruments fairly well, or paints a nice picture, but by virtue of spreading himself too thin, he will rarely be great at anything. Owners of such hands are generally inventive and love challenges and adventures; they are likely to belong to the class of people referred to as "Jack-of-all-trades." The linear pattern on the palm will further help to determine whether his versatility can be interpreted positively as brilliance and creativity, or negatively, indicating a lack of dependability and continuity. This will be discussed further in PART II of this book.

Bearers of such hands may find their "niche" as diplomats or in public relations, where an inborn versatility and adaptability will be an asset.

Figure 1, Elementary/Primitive Hand

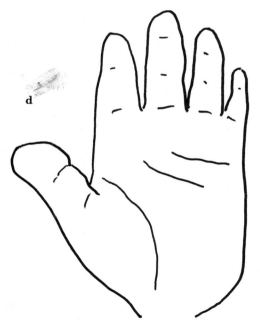

a) short stubby fingers and nails
b) few lines on palm
c) short thumb
d) bulbous thumb

Figure 2, Square/Useful Hand

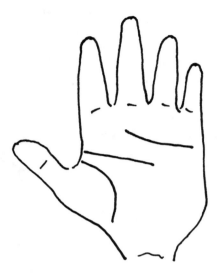

a) square palm
b) square fingers & finger setting
c) broad fingertips
d) broad/short nails

Figure 3, Spatulate/Energetic Hand

a) fingertips flared, wider at top

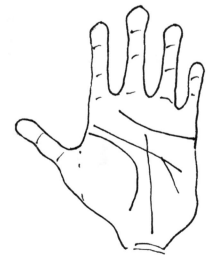

b) palm wider at wrist

c) palm wider at
   base of fingers

Figure 4, Philosophic/Intellectual Hand

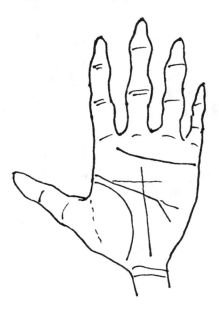

c) long finger nails

b) long bony fingers with
well-developed joints

a) long, angular palm

d) many additional
lines on palm

Figure 5, Conic/Artistic Hand

a) rounded palm
b) rounded/conic fingertips and nails
c) round setting of palm

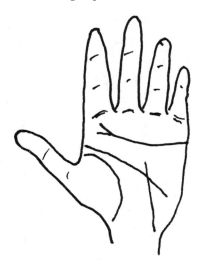

Figure 6, Psychic/Intuitive Hand

a) long narrow palm
b) long tapering, smooth fingers
c) long, almond-shaped nails

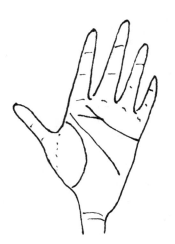

Figure 7, Mixed Hand

a) palm of any shape
b) fingers and tips of any shape
c) Ring of Saturn
d) many lines on palm

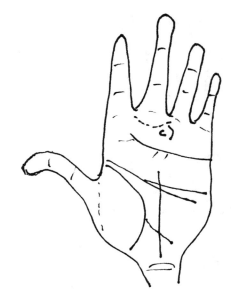

2

The Size of the Hand

SOMETIMES, LARGE HANDS AND FEET GO TOGETHER WITH A LARGE BODY-BUILD, but quite often, small people have surprisingly large hands, and vice-versa. The size of the hand does reveal interesting facts and gives many pointers to its owner's personality.

Whatever the actual size of a person's hand, it is overshadowed by the proportions between hand and fingers - width and length of the palm compared with the fingers - which constitute the special features that make a hand unique.

A man's hand may be considered average if it measures seven inches from the tip of the middle finger, which is usually the longest finger, to the wrist. Anything less or more is small, medium or large, but once again, the general build of the individual must be taken into consideration. A woman's glove size "six" is considered average, taking her general build and height into account as well. Now that we have discussed what is "average" let's discuss what "small" or "large" means.

Small Hands:

People whose hands are unusually small in comparison with the rest of their body THINK BIG AND ACT BIG. Have you ever noticed a small person getting out of an oversized car? Individuals with small hands can sum up strangers at a glance, and know instinctively if they can be trusted or not. They grasp the main points of a plan rapidly,

15

and are not afraid of making decisions. Therefore, such people prefer action, and they expect results, usually leaving the working-out of details to others, especially if the fingers are also short in comparison to the palm.

Small hands are found among every profession, but by virtue of their basic nature, these people gravitate toward work where their "take-charge" personalities are an asset, as in the business world. They should, and probably would not, choose a life where routine work is the main focus.

Large Hands:

Large hands, again by taking the person's build into account, reveal a thoughtful and analytical temperament. They belong to the individual who is deliberate and patient, not in a hurry to make up his mind about anything. It seems a strange paradox that people with large hands should be skilled in doing fine, delicate work. I once saw a pastry chef with the largest pair of hands doing intricate decorations.

Thick and Thin Hands:

Thickness is easy to judge. If there is any doubt look at the center of the palm while the fingers are stretched out. If the tendons are readily visible, the hand is thin. This is usually referred to as the "hollow palm," which reveals a reserved and somewhat introverted person. As always, this needs to be confirmed by numerous other indicators in the hand, such as flat or little-developed "mounts," or elevations, on the palmar surface. This will be fully discussed in Chapter 6.

The thicker the palm, the greater the physical stamina. Such people are usually active and possess much greater physical energy and vitality than those with thin palms. Thick hands are likely to be found among the Elementary, Square and Spatulate types, whereas thin ones go with the Philosophic and Psychic hands. The Conic/Artistic hand type may be either thin or fleshy.

Firm or Soft Hands:

A thick hand, firm to the touch, reveals stamina and vitality. A thick hand gone flabby and soft indicates a lack of physical activity, which reduces the vitality of which this person is capable.

If a hand is thick, hard and inflexible, it goes together with an inflexible and stubborn disposition; that individual has little sensitivity toward others. Thin hands show a measure of refinement. If they are thin and soft, this could be interpreted as self-indulgence and/or laziness. If thin and firm, the available energy is utilized to its greatest advantage.

Skin Texture:

When shaking or holding someone's hand, the texture is noticeable. Rough or smooth skin is not the result of hard manual work or the lack of it. People are born with this characteristic.

Silky, smooth skin hints at a fussy, exacting nature, which may well be over- critical, especially if the hand is long and bony. This points to a lack of empathy or feelings in general, especially if the "Mount of Venus" should be underdeveloped - discussed fully in Chapter 6.

Fine-textured skin is also a feature of the sensual personality, in which case the hand tends to be fleshy and soft rather than thin and bony. If the skin on the fingertips is smooth, regardless of the texture of the palm, its owner possesses inborn intuition.

Rough and coarse skin always indicates a lack of refinement. Hands of people who work in heavy industry may be callused and rough, but it does not alter the skin ridges. Those who are born with tough and leathery skin enjoy the simple, down-to-earth things in life, such as food, drink and sex.

The Handshake:

What can you tell from a handshake? Quite a lot. A hand that feels soft and fleshy tells us that its owner possesses a sensual, self-gratifying nature; he is fond of comforts and the good things in life. He may not want to work for luxuries himself, expecting others to provide them.

The cool hand is always ready to take rather than to give; it is likely to belong to the long and thin hand. Hot hands, unless the individual has a raging fever, reveal a spontaneous and impulsive nature with a tendency to be carried away by his moods. Warm-handed people have an approach to life similar to that of the hot-handed, but they are not as impulsive, although just as generous of spirit.

Robust health and energy, and an optimistic disposition, are shown by a handshake that is firm, yet elastic and springy. One that "crushes" you would indicate an overbearing disposition, one that could be insensitive toward others.

3

The Fingers

THE INDIVIDUAL FINGERS
(Figure 8)

THE NAMES GIVEN TO THE FINGERS ARE IN KEEPING WITH PALMISTRY'S LINK TO astrology, and are highly significant in their interpretation. Each finger rules or dominates over a particular sphere, and must first be considered separately, then in relation to the other fingers, and finally to the rest of the hand. The index finger is called JUPITER, or "world finger." The middle finger is SATURN, and is used as a gauge by which not only the other fingers but the length of the palm is measured. The ring finger is called APOLLO, the appreciator of beauty and harmony, and the little finger is MERCURY, the "messenger" of expression and communication.

THE PHALANGES
(Figure 9)

The fingers are divided into three sections called PHALANGES, which are treated individually in each finger. The sections are normally roughly equal in size, with the base phalange a fraction longer than the top and middle section. You will be surprised to see how differently proportioned these phalanges can be, giving special meaning to our preferences and tendencies.

19

- The first section is often referred to as the NAIL PHALANGE. It relates to the realm of mental and spiritual perceptions.
- The second or MIDDLE PHALANGE deals with our ability to find practical and viable solutions and applications for our ideas.
- The third or BASE PHALANGE reveals physical and instinc-tual needs, sets of values and traditions.

The Jupiter or Index Finger:

This finger shows how we see ourselves in relation to the world, and is therefore often referred to as the "world finger." It stands for "me," "myself" and "I." JUPITER is the finger of assertion, and is often used by people who are stressing a point; they point with this finger. A parent may admonish a child by wagging it back and forth. A short JUPITER finger is unlikely to be used in this fashion.

- If this finger is short by comparison to the 2nd and 3rd finger, the average reaching about the middle of the NAIL PHALANGE of SATURN, the person does not seek the leadership and respon-sibility for others. If overly long, the opposite is true.
- A long JUPITER finger on a broad, capable hand shows no fear of future or enterprise; a person is neither afraid of authority nor of exercising it.
- If a long JUPITER finger goes with a narrow, intuitive hand, it signifies a desire to dominate loved ones, out of fear of not being in control.
- If JUPITER leans toward SATURN, it often indicates introver-sion and an instinctive fear of the world. If extreme, it could even be an indication of "street fear." Leaning toward SATURN can also give a clue to a love of acquisitions, which constitutes a conscious or subconscious compensation for an inferiority com-plex.
- When the top or NAIL PHALANGE is short compared to the same sections of the other fingers, criticism from others is re-sented.
- Salesmen, teachers, and lecturers should have long and ta-pered first phalanges. This signifies a probing and inquiring type of mind.

- If the NAIL PHALANGE is square-tipped, its owner thrives on law and order, which would explain why it is often found among lawyers, judges and policemen.
- When the second or middle PHALANGE is long, the person is a great planner and organizer, making full use of his ideas - a great asset in the executive.
- When the third or BASE PHALANGE is large and firm, it shows physical domination over others and indicates "brawn rather than brain." This could be found in hands of animal trainers, foremen, etc.
- A flabby third phalange is a sign of excessive self-indulgence, where quantity rather than quality is desired.
- If one phalange is noticeably shorter than average, the positive values represented by that phalange are reduced. A short middle phalange of the JUPITER finger would show a lack of executive and planning abilities, or a preference toward a subordinate role.
- Rings worn on the right hand of the JUPITER finger announces loud and clear "I like to be in charge;" if worn on the left JUPITER finger, it indicates that such a person likes to be in charge at home or in his private life.
- A crooked or twisted index finger is not a good sign, unless it is caused by injury or arthritis. A long, crooked finger tells that its owner will go about achieving his aims in a devious or secretive fashion, or by using unscrupulous methods to get what he wants.

The Saturn or Middle Finger:

This is the most firmly rooted of all the fingers. It represents the serious part in man and is the keeper of law and order, home and stability. The SATURN finger should measure approximately 7/8 of the length of the palm to be considered average, which constitutes a good balance between seriousness and lightheadedness. This finger also serves as the gauge by which the other fingers are measured (see Figure 8).

- If the SATURN finger is of average length, the JUPITER and APOLLO fingers should reach halfway up the nail phalange (see Figure 8).

- When SATURN towers over the other fingers, it depicts a person who is overly serious, unable to see the bright side of things. Such an individual is sometimes referred to as "saturnine."
- When the fingers on either side seem to withdraw from SATURN, it indicates a tendency to be antisocial. If the tip of SATURN bends toward the third or APOLLO finger, a degree of introspection is revealed.
- A long nail phalange, especially if flexible at the first joint, signifies an interest in psychic phenomenon or psychic awareness. It may therefore be found in the hands of psychics, mediums or clairvoyants.
- If the second phalange dominates the finger, a strong tendency toward science and mathematics is indicated, but this is not restricted to those professions. Such long phalanges are also encountered among lovers of nature and farmers.
- When the third phalange is the dominant section, it points to someone with traditional values. If this section is long and thin, it may also reveal a liking of expensive home furnishings, but if long and broad, the bent is toward quantity rather than quality.
- If the third phalange is short and fat, the discriminating factor is absent and greed is indicated. When gaps are present at the bases of such fat third phalanges, the person has difficulty holding on to his cash. Normally, gaps between fingers are only evident if the base finger sections are thin.
- Knotty finger joints are an indication of a philosophical nature; they stem the flow of the impulses.
- A square fingertip of SATURN, regardless of the other fingertips, signifies an interest in legal matters, and for law and order in general.
- A spatulate fingertip adds a degree of inventiveness to the practicality.
- A fine or rounded fingertip reveals an affinity for numbers, which is excellent when found in the hand of an accountant.
- If rings are worn on this finger, whether on the left or right hand, it reveals a need for security.

The Apollo or Ring Finger:

Sometimes called the "Sun" or "Success" finger, APOLLO represents our instincts and personal relationships. The left or "private" APOLLO finger was chosen to wear marriage or engagementrings, symbolizing our intimate commitments.

The size, shape and position of APOLLO holds important information with regard to our basic attitudes. A well-developed APOLLO finger that reaches to the middle of the nail phalange of the SATURN finger, about the same length as JUPITER, reveals a person's appreciation of beauty and harmony in all forms, from nature to great works of art.

- If APOLLO pulls away from the SATURN finger, which represents the stability of home and traditions, the individual veers toward a more unorthodox lifestyle.

- If APOLLO leans towards SATURN, it signifies a need for security, and if it should even cling to the SATURN finger, it gives a clue to the person's excessive dependence on financial security.

- When the APOLLO finger is shorter than average (see Figure 8) or excessively short, it's owner has difficulty making decisions that involve risk-taking and does not like gambling in any shape or form. A person with an APOLLO finger that is shorter than average can still be successful, but he has to work hard for it because it won't fall into his lap.

- The opposite holds true if the APOLLO finger is much longer than average, occasionally even surpassing SATURN. Such a person is a risk-taker, especially if it should appear in the hand with an overly flexible bent-back thumb, further discussed in Chapter 4.

- If the fingertip section of APOLLO is long, the sense of the artistic is well-developed, especially if the tip is conic-rounded-in shape.

- When the first phalange is long and spatulate, broader at the tip, it indicates an inborn gift of story-telling and acting. To be a gifted actor, one should have a spatulate APOLLO fingertip. Such flared tips may be found among all professions, from tailors and carpenters to architects, and chances are that these people bring something special to their work.

- When the first phalange is long and broad, it signifies an ability to make money in a big way, overriding the aesthetic side.

- An actor or one who can mimic usually possesses a slender, longish second or middle phalange, which indicates quick responses and a ready wit, pays excellent attention to details, and has good color sense. If these traits are found in people who do not express themselves creatively, the analyst should suggest that they find an interest where their innate creativity can be expressed, because it would contribute much to their happiness and fulfillment.

- A long, slender third or BASE PHALANGE goes with a taste for decor and design, and reflects inborn good taste. A short and fat phalange would indicate the opposite, where the tendency would be toward quantity rather than quality.

- A long, broad third phalange which is firm and not flabby would reveal that its owner enjoys the good things in life, but not in excess. It could be found among connoisseurs of food and wine.

- A well-developed phalange of at least average length, coupled with a hand that is broad at the wrist shows a physically and mentally fit individual. This could belong to the athlete who has a positive attitude; he wants to win and feels confident with competition.

The Mercury or Little Finger:

This is the finger of "expression and communication." The size, shape and angle is indicative of honesty, inborn communication skills and practicality. The average-sized MERCURY reaches to the base of the nail phalange of the APOLLO finger (see Figure 8), unless it is set unusually low in the palm, which will be discussed later in this chapter in FINGER SETTINGS.

The MERCURY finger indicates our attitudes to relationships, but especially to our very first bonding with our parents. Any aberration in this finger could provide a clue to early problems in that area, such as a "twisted" finger (see Figure 10), which clearly reveals a lack of honesty or a "twisted mentality." These negative characteristics are often rooted in childhood experiences.

- People who possess a well-developed top phalange are natural teachers, salesmen, actors, public speakers and politicians; in short, anyone who makes the art of communication his or her profession.

- When the nail phalange is the longest of the three sections, and tapered, such a person can be especially persuasive, and even more so if this finger leans toward the APOLLO finger. Such a person wouldn't mind stretching a point in order to reach his aim. This long, tapering finger is also referred to as the "finger of enterprise" because it indicates quick responses.

- Rounded tips on the MERCURY finger are an indication of good communication and language skills.

- Knotty, well-developed finger joints on MERCURY - as in the other fingers - show love of law and order. Since knotty joints stop the flow of impulses and spontaneity, they reflect careful, analytical thinking.

- If the entire MERCURY finger is broad and sturdy, its owner is generally broad-minded with a live-and-let-live attitude.

- A long, knotty, thin finger of MERCURY sitting on a broad palm says that its owner is not easily aroused sexually, while such a finger on a thin, dry palm indicates a lack of sexual interest.

- When the top and second phalanges are pressed in toward the APOLLO finger, it indicates a self-indulgent nature, especially if the third or base phalange is fat and puffy.

- When the third phalange is enlarged on the inside of the finger toward the APOLLO finger (see Figure 11), it indicates a conflict of loyalties between parents or siblings and his acquired later family, such as spouse and children.

- If one marriage partner has such a "stepped-in" formation, he or she will always have split loyalties between parents and wife/husband. It is therefore an unfavorable feature. When found in the hands of a young person, it reveals a desire to fly the nest, but a sense of obligation toward his parents may not let him go.

THE FINGERTIPS

(Figure 12, a-d)

There are four basic shapes of fingertips: the tapered/pointed, the conic/rounded, the square, and the spatulate/flared.

One person may not have the same fingertips on all of his fingers, but it would be unusual to have extreme shapes together in one hand, such as very tapered mixed with either square or spatulate first phalanges. Such opposites may be encountered in the "Mixed hand."

The Tapered Tips:

With the tapered or pointed fingertips, the energy flow enters uninterrupted, and are often referred to as the "psychic" fingertips. People possessing these are quick in perceptions and responses. They can absorb impressions very rapidly, often without being conscious of it. As a rule, these individuals pay meticulous attention to details, and may be "wrapped up" in them rather than with the main issue. Patience and attention to details seems to be a trademark of the tapered fingertips.

The Rounded Fingertips:

People with rounded/conic fingertips have a personality that works smoothly and without friction. They always need beauty and harmony in their surroundings for maximum development of the individual's potential. These people are generally socially oriented, and their inborn sense of balance and dislike of friction extends to all of their relationships.

The Square Fingertips:

When entering a square fingertip, the energy has to slow down. Square tips, therefore, reveal a mind that is practical and deliberate. The mentality associated with square tips is an analytical one; this individual seeks practical solutions to a problem or situation. Such a person will focus on his work with a singlemindedness that makes him an excellent craftsman in any profession, from cabinet maker to plastic surgeon or dentist.

The Flared or Spatulate Fingertips:

The energy has to break down the greatest resistance when entering this type of fingertip, which creates friction, agitation and excitement. The person with this kind of fingertip should have some physical outlet, because he possesses an abundance of physical and nervous energy; at best, this energy should be discharged creatively in the form of challenges for the body and mind. People with spatulate shapes of hands and fingertips are endowed with individuality and originality, but they are not known for patience. They do not accept conventional answers, which makes them appear "pig-headed" and obstinate at times.

If individuals with spatulate fingertips choose the teaching profession, they could be exciting teachers, because they would have the ability to stimulate and awaken unusual ideas in those they come in contact with.

THE FINGER SETTING

It is important to notice how the fingers "sit" on the palm. There are four basic settings, described below. A good way to determine these is to make an outline of the hand, and with a ruler draw a line from the JUPITER to the MERCURY finger across the palm.

The Uneven Setting: (Figure 13)

This is the most common finger setting; the JUPITER and SATURN fingers are almost level with each other. The APOLLO finger drops down slightly, and MERCURY is lower than the others. When the MERCURY finger crouches very low on the palm, this implies that its owner chooses a difficult approach to life. A low MERCURY restricts the ability to communicate, especially in terms of affection. In many hands, this finger would be quite tall, but by virtue of its setting it appears shorter than average. A low-set MERCURY reduces the good qualities ascribed to this finger. One of the interpretations of such a setting is that its bearer has been unable, in some area, to reach his full potential. It seems a paradox that a number of writers and poets are said to have such low-set Mercury fingers, probably because they are able to say in writing what they cannot express in the spoken language.

Both hands must be checked for the finger setting, as they may reveal variations that would be meaningful.

The Square Setting: (Figure 14)

If the fingers are set squarely on the palm, there is no lack of confidence. On the contrary, it may border on arrogance. Since such a person believes himself to be invincible and infallible, he usually achieves his goals. In the hands of salesmen, coupled with strong Mercury and Jupiter fingers, this setting means that success is almost assured. The negative side of this square setting is that such a person could be unbearable in his over-confident and know-it-all demeanor.

The Rounded Setting: (Figure 15)

When the fingers are set in a gentle arch, it signifies a good mental balance. Such people are neither arrogant, nor do they suffer from lack of confidence. They are generally good communicators. One sees that type of finger setting often in the Conic/Artistic hand. These people avoid unnecessary confrontations, but if necessary, they will stand up for what they believe.

Low-Set Jupiter and Mercury Fingers: (Figure 16)

When both Jupiter and Mercury fingers are set low, it indicates problem areas, especially since Jupiter represents the ego, and a low setting would point to a lack of self-esteem. Such a person may feel that he lacks control over his life. If a low-set Jupiter is restricted to the left or "private" hand, these feelings of low esteem may be confined to his intimate life; if in the right hand only, it would involve his profession, but if it appears in both, this lack of confidence would permeate his entire personality.

FLEXIBILITY VERSUS INFLEXIBILITY

Flexible fingers are synonymous with a flexible mind. People who possess them are unconventional and inquisitive. Security and position are not of great importance to them. On the negative side, they may let opportunities or cash slip easily through these flexible fingers.

Fingers that bend at the top joint indicate a tolerant attitude toward others. This would also reveal an innate intuition and understanding, while the pliable second joint reflects a flexibility of a more down-to-earth, practical nature.

When the fingers bend back like rubber, such an individual is very impressionable, with a tendency to be open-minded, but also "open-mouthed;" he or she likes gossip.

The opposite holds true if the fingers are extremely stiff and un-bending, which goes hand in hand with a rigid disposition; these people have little use for social amenities.

Fingers that turn in toward the palm show a cautious and often insecure personality, while a hand with widely spaced fingers reveals an adventurous and optimistic attitude.

Figure 8, The Hand and Finger Proportions

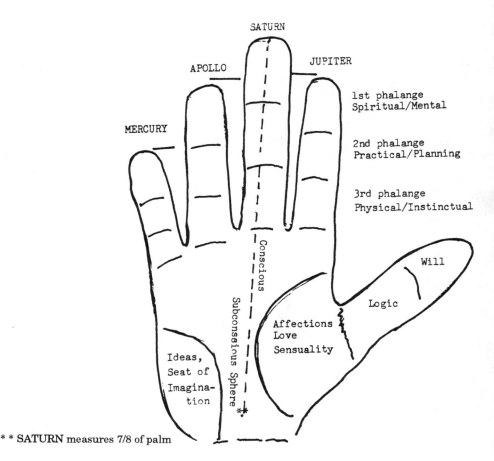

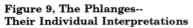

**Figure 9, The Phlanges--
Their Individual Interpretations**

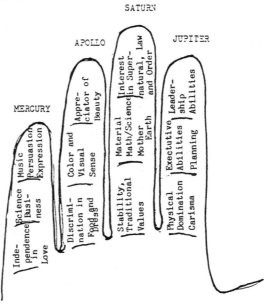

Figure 10, Twisted MERCURY Finger

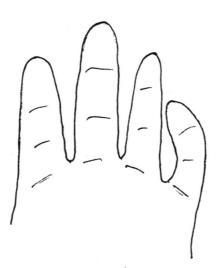

Figure 11, Enlarged MERCURY Finger on Inside

Figure 12, The Basic Fingertips

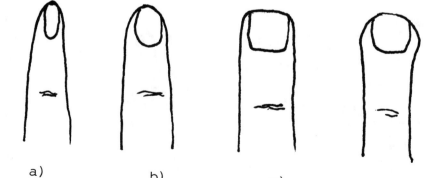

a)
tapered

b)
round

c)
square

d)
spatulate

Figure 13, The "Uneven" Finger Setting

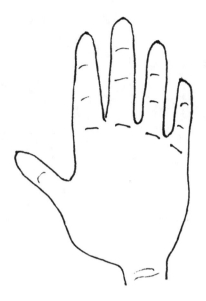

Figure 14, The Square Finger Setting

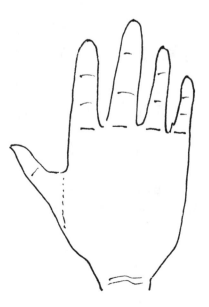

Figure 15, The "Rounded" Setting

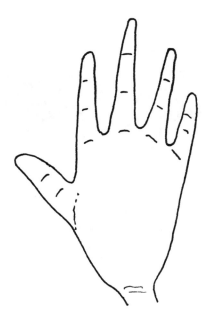

Figure 16, Low-Set Jupiter and Mercury Fingers

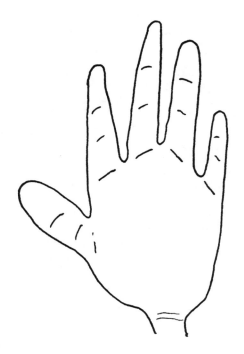

4

The Thumb

THE THUMB IS ALSO A FINGER, BUT IT IS INFINITELY MORE THAN THAT. IT IS extremely important to us, and if injured or worse, we realize how lost we are without it. According to anthropologists, the thumb "individualizes man." They claim that as ape evolved into man, he used the thumb for holding and throwing stones, then manufacturing tools, utensils and fine instruments. An imprint of an ape's hand would be quite similar to that of man, except that it is characterized by a very small and low-set thumb, bent toward the palm. The logical deduction is that the stronger and better-proportioned the thumb, the higher evolved the individual.

In the East, where the science of palmistry was studied many centuries ago, some scholars devoted their entire time to the study of the thumb, claiming that it holds all the answers to an individual's personality and health. One of these scholars coined the phrase that "the thumb is to the palmist what the North Star is to the navigator."

Early midwives watched newborn babies very closely, which included the thumb. If the hand remained closed up with the thumb inside for too many days, they started to get concerned about the mental and physical well-being of the child. If a person clenches his hands over the thumbs, or even hides them like a newly-born, it signifies an instinctive fear.

THE SECTIONS OF THE THUMB
(Figure 17)

There are three sections or phalanges to the thumb. The first or nail phalange refers to the WILL of the person, and also to his mental qualities, just as do the other fingers.

The second or middle phalange represents the LOGIC and powers of rationalization, and of relating and implementing ideas.

The third section of the thumb forms the base of the Mount of Venus, which will be discussed in detail in Chapter 6, - THE MOUNTS OR ELEVATIONS. This third phalange embraces the physical aspect of love and affection.

THE LENGTH OF THE THUMB

The thumb of average length, (Figure 17) reaches to the middle of the base phalange of the JUPITER finger, when measured against it. The length of the thumb can be deceiving, depending on whether it is set low or high on the hand. A person whose thumb is set low, starting almost from the wrist, lives more by instinct than by logic, but it is the overall length and strength that tells how capable, determined and persistent its owner is. The thumb resembles the root of a tree. If sturdy and powerful, it conveys these qualities to man. Such a person will endure even in the face of adversities.

- The man with a short, clumsy, low-set or bulbous thumb (Figures 1 d and 27) is himself coarse, brutish, and animal-like in his behavior. This kind of thumb belongs to the elementary or primitive hand type, although its variations may be found among other hand types as well.
- The opposite holds true with long, well-shaped and well-proportioned thumbs. Such people possess inborn refinement, and use their intellect rather than brute force to achieve their goals.
- When the thumb sections are unevenly developed, as for instance the first phalange very long in contrast to the second, it depicts a person who depends on his WILL rather than LOGIC. Consequently, he would have a tendency to be impulsive and make rash decisions.

- When the second phalange is much longer than the first, the individual lacks decisive qualities; this thumb is often referred to as the "Hamlet Thumb" - "to be or not to be." If this second phalange is thin and streamlined, it is called the "wasted thumb," which indicates tact and refinement in those who possess it.
- If the third phalange, which forms the base of the Mount of Venus, is over-developed in comparison to the other two sections, or to the hand itself, such a person is the victim of his own passion and inborn sensuality of nature.

THE SHAPES OF THE THUMB

There are many variations in the shapes of thumbs. The best way to determine this is by making an outline of the thumb you are examining.

The Thick-Set, Sturdy Thumb: (Figure 18)

This type of thumb generally belongs to people whose approach to problems and dealing with others is direct and forthright. This characteristic can border on stubbornness and tactlessness, depending on the stiffness and thickness of the thumb. This kind of thumb quite often belongs to the Square/Practical or the Spatulate/Energetic hand types.

The Slender Thumb: (Figure 19)

A slender and high-set thumb usually goes with the Intellectual/ Philosophic, Conic/Artistic or Psychic/Intuitive hand types. This shaped thumb reflects a certain finesse, and belongs to a person who has the ability to be diplomatic and tactful, especially if the second thumb section has the "wasted" look, meaning that it is graceful and streamlined.

The Arched Thumb: (Figure 20)

This type of thumb is the opposite of the thick-set, sturdy thumb. It indicates versatility and flexibility, and when bent away from the hand at an extreme angle, it reveals a tendency toward gambling and risk taking. Such a person has difficulty holding on to his cash.

The "Musical" Thumb: (Figure 21)

According to David Brandon-Jones in his book "Practical Palmistry," people with this kind of thumb possess an inborn sense of timing and rhythm. Speaking from my own experience, I attended a large family gathering and was able to observe that the branch of the family known for musical talent and excellent rhythm in dancing all possessed this type of thumb, with the acute angle at the base joint.

THE TIPS OF THE THUMB

The nail phalange with its thumb tip symbolizes the WILL of the individual. Without the benefit of a strong thumb tip of at least average length, the abilities of an individual may not be fully realized.
As an example, an average-sized thumb with a short first section and an excessively long second phalange belongs to a person who has difficulty making decisions, and therefore often misses opportunities.

The opposite holds true with a disproportionally long tip section, which indicates that its owner makes his decisions based only on his will and not on logical deductions.

There are many different thumb tips and variations. Below are the most basic types with regard to shapes and fullness, or the lack of it.

- A well-padded thumb tip shows a reservoir of physical and mental energy. Such a person is usually in control of himself and does not easily lose his composure, but when he does, watch out.
- The flattened thumb tip (Figure 22) reflects a person who thrives on nervous energy but loses steam quickly. When the energy is depleted, he or she has to lie-low until his stamina is available for new challenges.
- The long and broad thumb tip (Figure 23) generally belongs to the person with executive power, one who has the ability and desire to command men. If these qualities are in excess, so is the person's need to be in absolute command.
- If any of these strong thumbs are reinforced by a ledge on the back of the thumb (Figure 24), it reflects extreme stubbornness. Such a person is so opinionated that ideas other than his own stand a small chance of coming across.

- A long and thin thumb tip (Figure 25) is the opposite of the above. Such an individual would be content to direct the action from the side line rather than joining the work force.

- While a broad top joint of the thumb indicates keen mentality, the thumb that ends in a pointed tip (Figure 26) shows a person who concentrates with razor-sharp persistence on a target. He will not quit until he has accomplished his goals or intentions.

- A coarse, heavy-looking thumb tip belongs to a person who lacks tact and diplomacy, and especially self-control. The extreme shape of this thumb (Figure 27) is often called the "murderer's thumb." One would expect this type of thumb to belong to the most primitive and elementary hand type, and it usually does, but it is also found among any of the other categories. Wherever it makes its appearance, it is a sign of a "hot" and sometimes ungoverned temper.

- The conic/rounded thumb tip shows good taste and a discriminating personality (Figure 12 b). Unlike the "arrowhead-tip" described in Figure 26, the rounded tip belongs to people who are adventurous and love variety.

- Square tips generally belong to the Square hand type, described in Chapters 1 and 3. (Figure 12 c) People with such thumb tips use the common sense approach to life, but unlike those with "stubborn" thumb tips, as described in Figures 23 and 24, these people are willing to listen to someone else's point of view.

- The spatulate tip (Figure 12 d) is most likely to be found with the Spatulate/Energetic hand type. As described in Chapters 1 and 3, they belong to the most individualistic and innovative brand of people.

FLEXIBILITY AND RESISTANCE

These characteristics are almost as much "national traits" as they are individual ones. More supple thumbs are found among the Eastern cultures and Latin nations than in Northern Europe. Such national prototypes of thumbs show the influence of climate over thousands of years on the physical and emotional development of the inhabitants.

In the United States, which is a melting pot for all nations, a variety of thumb tips are in evidence, from the very supple to the stiff jointed varieties.

The Supple Thumb:

The supple, as well as the double-jointed thumb, which bends back from the hand at an extreme angle is that of an extravagant person, not only in matters of money, which such people find hard to hold onto, but also with regard to their lifestyle. They possess adaptable temperaments, and adjust relatively quickly to new surroundings and situations.

The Firm-Jointed Thumb:

Almost the opposite holds true for the firm- or stiff-jointed thumb. Such people take the practical rather than extravagant route, and they are more cautious about getting into new ventures. They are also less versatile than the supple-jointed person. A good, firm thumb is an asset to have. Such individuals are dependable and loyal, but not demonstrative in their affections.

The stiff-jointed thumb is the extreme type and belongs to people who are unyielding and inflexible in their outlook on life.

Depending on the rest of the hand, a firm thumb is often needed to lend stability, or give balance to a hand that otherwise lacks firmness, as in a soft and pliable hand.

Check For Resistance:

A good test for the analyst is to press against the thumb of the person he is evaluating. The thumb that offers resistance indicates a quality of control that its owner has over himself. If the thumb is of the flexible type and possesses the "money-spending-arch," the lack of mobility at its base is an excellent feature, for it holds the extravagance in check.

Figure 17, The Thumb Sections

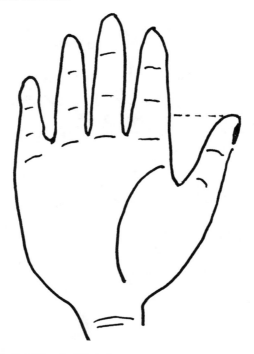

Figure 18, The Thick-Set Sturdy Thumb

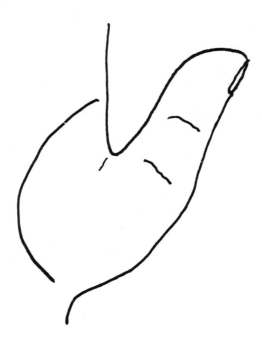

Figure 19, The Slender Thumb

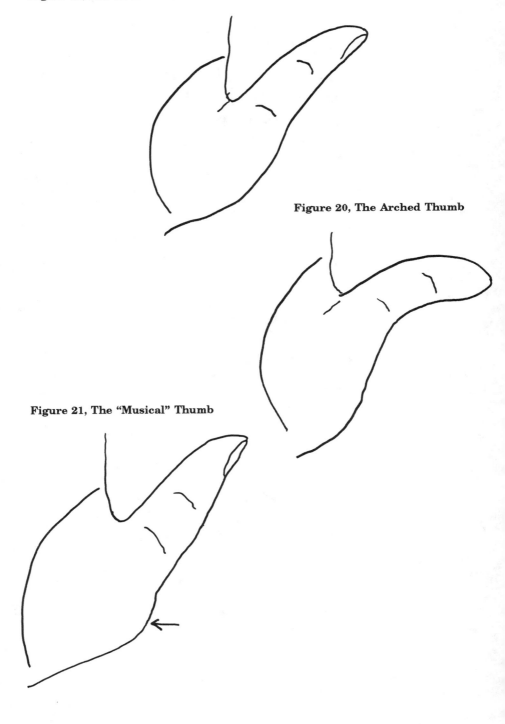

Figure 20, The Arched Thumb

Figure 21, The "Musical" Thumb

THE THUMB TIPS

**Figure 22,
Flat Thumb**

**Figure 23,
Long, Strong Tip**

**Figure 24,
Stubborn Ledge**

**Figure 25,
Long, Slender Tip**

**Figure 26,
"Arrowhead" Tip**

**Figure 27,
"Murder's" Thumb**

5

The Nails

THE FINGER AND THUMB NAILS PROVIDE VALUABLE INFORMATION NOT ONLY WITH regard to a person's vitality, but to his present state of health, character and temperament.

The length of the nail from the cuticle to the fingertip, without the nail extensions that women are so proud of, should measure about half of the nail phalange to be considered of average length.

- Shorter than average nails (Figure 28) are indicative of a personality that is full of "vim and vigor." People with such nails are quick-witted, and quite often have a temper to match. They possess an inborn tendency to be critical of others and themselves. There is no doubt that short-nailed individuals are the "doers" and not the "dreamers."
- When the nails are broader than long, tension and frustration, often created by the individuals themselves, are increased, with the result that they may bite their nails. It is small wonder that they also have a tendency to develop stomach problems due to inner stress (Figure 28). Such nails are likely to be encountered among the Spatulate and Square hand types, rather than the Philosophic or Psychic.
- If the nails are extremely short and small (Figure 29), the individual has a parsimonious nature, to say the least. This will

45

be reflected in his narrow lifestyle, and if small nails are found on square-tipped fingers, the person leads a dull and unadventurous life.

- Nails that are about as broad as they are long (Figure 30) belong to people with a dependable and honest personality. Due to an inborn sense of loyalty, they make excellent friends. Such people are also practical and resourceful. These nails may be found among many of the hand types, but are rarely seen on the Psychic/Intuitive hands, which are characterized by long, almond-shaped nails (Figure 32).

- Dish-shaped nails (Figure 31) are not a sign of robust health. They may have taken on this shape after having experienced trauma, or it may be the result of continuous tension. Such people should avoid stressful situations as much as possible, and ought to be watching their diets.

- People with long, oval-shaped nails (Figure 32) have less natural energy than those with broad-shaped nails, which does not imply that they are sickly. Their disposition is more placid, with the result that they don't use up much energy. One of the features of long, slender nails is patience with details and people. These characteristics would be well applied in the teaching profession.

- The above described nails should not be mistaken for nails that are very narrow, and quite often curl over, resembling talons of birds of prey. (Figure 33) Individuals with such nails are out for themselves, and will spot opportunities that will benefit them with an eagle eye.

THE COLOR OF NAILS

Nails that are a lively pink color are a sign of good health. If the color deepens to red however, it is too much of a good thing, for it reveals an agitated disposition that turns quickly to anger.

The opposite holds true if the nails are grayish or white, which indicates a lack of energy and vitality. If the nails have a bluish tint, it shows poor circulation.

THE TEXTURE OF THE NAILS

Nails that are smooth, with semi-circular "moons" showing at the base of the fingernails are a sign of good health. If the nails have vertical ridges, it indicates a nervous disposition, or it could be the result of a shock. If the nails are grooved horizontally, this points to a past infection or illness. Since it takes from six to nine months for a nail to grow out, you can calculate when the illness occurred. A similar situation is the appearance of white specks in the fingernails, which give a clue to a nervous disposition at the time. As with horizontal ridges, these specks may appear at a particular time of stress in a person's life, and will disappear when the nail grows out.

SHAPES OF FINGER NAILS

Figure 28

Figure 29

Figure 30

Figure 31

Figure 32

Figure 33

6

The Mounts

THE MAP OF THE MOUNTS
(Figure 34)

As you can see from the chart, there are eight mounts or elevated points on the palmar surface.

Each finger mount is located under the finger bearing its name. The thumb area has two mounts: the large MOUNT OF VENUS that forms the root of the thumb and is encircled by the Life line, and the smaller mount called the MOUNT OF LOWER MARS, which lies just above the MOUNT OF VENUS and below the MOUNT OF JUPITER. The MOUNT OF UPPER MARS is situated across the palm under the MOUNT OF MERCURY, and above the large MOUNT OF LUNA, the seat of our instincts and imagination.

FULL OR FLAT MOUNTS

To judge whether the mounts are elevated or flat, the hand to be examined must be relaxed and lean slightly forward. This will show the elevations and depressions more clearly. Generally speaking, if the finger mounts are well-developed, so will be the MOUNTS of VE-NUS and LUNA, but there are many exceptions, and a lack of development in one area and over-developed in another are often noticed; these features must not be overlooked when examining a hand.

Fullness of the mounts indicates vitality, energy, and the capacity for warmth and love, especially if it applies to the Mounts of VENUS, JUPITER and APOLLO. Exaggeration does not signify an increase of these good qualities, rather the opposite. Excess is never a good thing; it could reveal that the owner of the hand is at the mercy of his own instincts and desires.

THE MOUNT OF VENUS

This mount lies in the conscious, but passive half of the hand, which will be further discussed in PART IV, Chapter 2. The width and depth of this mount measures our capacity to give and receive emotional warmth, love and sensuality. When small, flat and also hard, the individual lacks these qualities. If the entire palm is thin and fleshless, like an arid wasteland, with a pallid color, it reveals a lack of physical resources.

THE MOUNT OF LUNA

This mount is situated across from the MOUNT OF VENUS, and is in the unconscious instinctive zone. It is the seat of our ideas, creativity and imagination and represents our "ID," which is the nucleus of our entire personality.

A flat mount would indicate a decrease of the above mentioned characteristics, but when over-developed, it could have worse ramifications. Such a person would be unrealistic in his sentiments and ideas, which could lead to hero and cult worship to various degrees.

THE MOUNT OF JUPITER

As the finger of Jupiter stands for ambition and achievement, a well-padded mount increases the good qualities credited to that sphere. (Chapter 3) A long and strong Jupiter finger with an equally well-developed mount reveals the desire to be in charge or command, but an overlong finger and an excessively high mount indicates that the person **must** be in charge, in which case, leadership could turn to tyranny. Whether such a person would apply physical force or overambitiousness on an intellectual plane would largely depend on the hand type. People of the more earthy and fiery Square and Spatulate hand types, respectively, would have a greater tendency toward physical domination than the Philosophic/Intellectual types.

THE MOUNT OF SATURN

This finger is the dividing line between the conscious and unconscious spheres. If SATURN and its mount are well-proportioned - neither too long nor too short, flat or exaggerated - it reveals good balance between the serious and lightheartedness of its owner. But if the finger is abnormally long, and the mount in excess, this could signify a morbid and somber nature.

A flat or little-elevated mount indicates disappointment in some area in the person's life; it would be most likely in the private sector, since the domain of the SATURN finger is "home and stability."

THE MOUNT OF APOLLO

This mount is situated in the unconscious zone of the hand. When well-developed, it reflects inborn appreciation of all things beautiful and harmonious, be it as a nature or art lover, or in the realm of literature and poetry. Whether the person has an avocation, or is an active creator of art will be confirmed by the rest of the hand. In either case, a well-padded MOUNT OF APOLLO with a finger of at least average length promises a degree of refinement and tact.

- When the mount is flat with a shorter than average finger, the opposite holds true. Such a person gets little enjoyment out of the beauty that surrounds him.
- When the Apollo finger is longer than average with an excessively high mount, it reveals a tendency toward gambling and extravagance.

THE MOUNT OF MERCURY

This mount is also situated in the unconscious sphere of the hand, and tells of our inborn inclinations toward adventure. Since Mercury is the sphere that rules over communication of all kinds, this also extends to intimate relationships.

A well-developed mount- and finger of at least average length - shows a healthy appetite for excitement, love of travel, etc., provided that the finger is not bent or twisted, in which case the favorable qualities ascribed to it would decrease, because a high mount with such a finger is an indication of a twisted and dishonest mentality.

THE MOUNT OF LOWER MARS

This mount is located directly above the MOUNT OF VENUS, and lies in the conscious sector of the hand. If well-developed, it reflects physical courage and mental daring. Such a person will possess a fighting spirit, perseverance and staying power, provided that the hand also has a strong thumb and favorable lines of Heart and Head, discussed in PART II - Chapter 2. If this mount is exaggerated and bulging, it gives a clue to an aggressive nature; this individual wouldn't need much encouragement to start an argument or fight.

If this mount is flat or absent, it shows a lack of courage; such a person takes the passive approach in life. The absence of this mount is more often encountered in the Psychic/Intuitive hand type, which is already more yielding by nature, whereas the Practical/Useful and Spatulate/Energetic types would be more likely to show a developed MOUNT OF LOWER MARS.

THE MOUNT OF UPPER MARS

This mount lies in the unconscious zone of the hand directly below the MOUNT OF MERCURY and measures our passive and instinctive courage. It also reveals whether the ideas and daring promised in the MOUNT OF LOWER MARS are being realized. A completely flat or undeveloped mount with a high MOUNT OF LOWER MARS would indicate that such a person does not have the staying power to carry out his ideas, in which case it would simply be reflective of an argumentative and aggressive nature.

If this area of UPPER MARS is well-developed, the outer edge of the hand called "percussion" will bulge, which quite often belongs to the resourceful and ingenious personality.

Figure 34,
Map of the Mounts

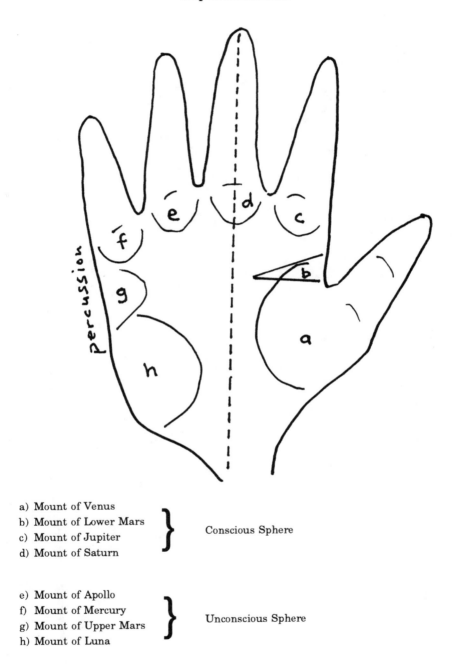

a) Mount of Venus
b) Mount of Lower Mars
c) Mount of Jupiter
d) Mount of Saturn

⎱ Conscious Sphere

e) Mount of Apollo
f) Mount of Mercury
g) Mount of Upper Mars
h) Mount of Luna

⎱ Unconscious Sphere

PART TWO

Palmistry

☆

A comprehensive manual for scientific palmistry.
Dactyloglyphics, the patterns formed on fingertips and
the palmar surface; lines, and other markings.

7

The Major Lines in the Hand

THE LINES OF LIFE, HEAD AND HEART ARE CONSIDERED BY ALL SCHOOLS OF palmistry to be the major ones. Everybody possesses a Life line, but apparently this is not the case with the others, and sometimes the Head and Heart lines melt together into one called the SIMIAN line, which will be discussed later in this chapter.

These major lines are formed during the first sixteen weeks of pregnancy and are part of our genetic code. They are generally the most prominent and deepest of all the lines, and, by virtue of their placement, cover every sphere of the palm.

It is of utmost significance to observe the starting and ending points of these lines, for this varies greatly from one person to another, which makes our hands so unique.

THE LIFE LINE

This is considered the number-one-line. (Figure A, Map of Palm). Most people associate it with "length of life," which is not entirely correct. They will come up to me holding out their hand and ask one question, "How long will I live?" Although it is one of the lines from which an approximate time frame can be obtained, it is a far greater yardstick with regard to a person's vitality and health. This is indicated by its smoothness, depth and color.

The Color and Depth:

The color and depth are important features to observe in the lines, especially with regard to the major ones.

- If the color is pink and the line well-marked, it indicates vitality and resistance to physical and psychological reverses.
- If the line is deep, but not trench-like, it reveals strong emotions and positive responses. Such a person is blessed with a natural endurance, and once he is set on a course, he will usually pursue it.
- If the line is thin, fragile and barely visible, it signifies the opposite of the above qualities. The lack of vitality is often due to decreased physical energy.

The Second Life Line:

Occasionally, a hand shows two life lines that run separate courses, i.e., an inner and outer circle. This indicates that such people lead two different kinds of lives, as the case of an actor whose professional life is "public property," so to speak, while he could be a recluse at heart who gingerly protects his private domain from observation.

The Starting Points:

Usually, the Life line starts at the edge of the hand about halfway between the insertion of the thumb and the Mount of Jupiter (see Map, Figure 35). If this line has a chained or weak beginning, with the result that the line would be barely visible, it reflects physical problems, usually from the moment of birth; as the child gets stronger, so will the line.

When the Life line swings out naturally in a wide circle, it indicates an adventurous nature and extroverted personality, at least one who prefers variety. If, on the other hand, the line hugs the thumb closely and forms a narrow path around the Mount of Venus, the hand belongs to a socially timid and cautious individual.

The Influence Line: (Figure 36 f)

When a thinner line accompanies the Life parallel to it on the inside, it is called an "Influence line," and is a favorable sign, for it indicates resistance to illnesses and infections. Such a person would have a good immune system. This line must not be confused with another line in the same area which is called the "Mars line" (see Map, Figure 35 g-g), which will be discussed in the next chapter.

Forks on the Life Line: (Figure 36, a-d)

If the Life line has a distinct branch veering off in another direction, it indicates that its owner likes variety, and the direction will tell you of its nature.

- If the branch swerves toward the Mount of Luna, the person likes travel and adventure, but if the main line continues its course around the thumb, it reveals that he always loves to come home to "roost." (Figure 36 a).
- If a branch from the Life line veers toward the Mount of Jupiter, it signifies ambition and a desire for leadership; this branch is therefore sometimes referred to as the AMBITION line. Goals mean different things to different people; one person's greatest dream or ambition may be to learn to fly, while another's may be to become a senator or own a restaurant. The stronger this branch line, and the closer it reaches its destination, the Mount of Jupiter, the better are a person's chances for realization. (Figure 36 b).
- If a branch leaves the Life line in the direction of SATURN, it is sometimes called the EFFORT line. If this person becomes successful, it would be through his own endeavors. (Figure 36 c).
- If a branch from the Life line travels toward the Mount of Apollo and actually reaches it, it is referred to as the SUCCESS line, but most of the time, this is achieved through a person's own effort. As the saying goes: "A person makes his own luck." (Figure 36 d).

Interruptions of the Life Line: (Figure 36 e)

If the Life line is interrupted at some point during its course, but continues with a new line forming between the two ends, it indicates a change in the person's life style. If the line after the interruption is stronger or continues in a wider circle, the change was a favorable one.

THE HEAD LINE

This is often referred to as the "Line of Mentality." Palmists consider this the second most important line, but only because without the Life line a person would not exist!

The Head line gives a clue to our reasoning and mental capacity by virtue of its length, depth, starting and ending points. It is also very important that this line be relatively free of markings such as islands, dots and frazzles, which will be discussed in detail later in this chapter.

As to the color and depth of the line, the same characteristics apply as with the Life line.

It is of utmost significance that both hands of a person be examined in order to observe possible changes from the left, or "birth" hand to the right, or "dominant" hand, if right-handed, and vice versa if left-handed. For instance, if the Head line in the left hand is short and wavy, but longer and straighter, or with added forks, in the right hand, it is an indication that such an individual has come far in developing his potential. This is usually confirmed by other findings in the hand.

The Starting Points:

These are of paramount importance because they reveal a person's basic, inborn attitudes and outlook on life at a glance. (Figure 37, a-f).

- If the Head line starts with the Life line (Figure 37 a), just slightly touching it at the beginning, such people are by nature cautious and moderate. They have a tendency to keep traditions and seldom go to extremes, and are neither overly aggressive nor gullible.

- If the lines of Life and Head are tightly meshed together at the beginning, (Figure 37 b), and also follow the same course for a distance, it reveals more than average caution. Such a person is ultra-sensitive toward criticism, and is very concerned what others think and feel about him. Because of a lack of self-confidence, he does not handle failures very well. (Figure 37 b).

I recently examined the hands of a person with a doctorate of philosophy, about 63 years old, and was surprised to see this formation as described above in his RIGHT HAND, whereas the left or "birth" hand was different in that the lines of Life and Head barely touched at the beginning, and then separated. I expressed my surprise to him, for this lack of independence did not otherwise repeat itself in his hand. He told me that this was no surprise to him, because he had an extremely domineering mother who would not let him live his own life, and was also very critical of him. He went into the Military Service, and while on an R & R furlough in San Francisco, he fell in love. They got married without his mother's knowledge. Needless to say the mother was furious, but she could do nothing to stop the "fait accompli."

- If the Head line starts inside the Life line on the Mount of Lower Mars, (Figure 37 c), it shows a personality that is extremely sensitive to criticism, coupled with the excitability and aggression which is inherited from the Mount of Lower Mars. It is obvious that this is not a favorable starting point to possess, but if the line emerges from its "prison" and takes a fairly straight course across the palm, this person has overcome unfavorable tendencies by adding common sense and self-control, which are a clue to a well-functioning personality. (Figure 37 c). If however, the line of Head shows weakness after this negative beginning, or if it continues on a far too descending course toward the center of the palm (Figure 37 c), it would indicate that such a person has not been able to lift himself up and is at the mercy of his initial handicap.

Remember that we all start out in life with positive and negative characteristics. How some people are able to extricate themselves from bad breaks in life while others cannot, and how some are born with all possible advantages and ruin their chances, is an ever-intriguing puzzle that is hard to explain.

- If the Head line is separated from the Life line by a small margin (Figure 37 e), self-reliance, independence of thought and quick judgement are reflected. Such people have no problems making decisions, and it is not surprising that they often display leadership abilities.

- If this separation between the Head and Life lines is wide, (Figure 37 f), it is considered an excess of the above mentioned qualities. Quickness in decision-making may turn into rashness and impulsiveness, and courage becomes recklessness. Such people would benefit from possessing a strong thumb as a balance. Having such a wide separation of the two major lines, an overly flexible thumb and smooth fingers, without developed joints, would only enhance the negative characteristics.

The Course of the Head Line:

According to Cheiro, the famous 19th Century palmist, it is of utmost importance to realize that different hand types come equipped with different Head lines. On a Square hand, a straight line is "normal," while on the Psychic/Intuitive, the normal course is an inclination toward the Mount of Luna. Therefore, if one sees a very sloping Head line on the Square hand, it is a strange paradox. This would signify the addition of imagination and creativity to the basically materialistic and practical personality, but if the line should be slanting excessively, or even terminate on the Mount of Luna, it would not be a favorable sign. In such a case, the person would have a morbid imagination with a tendency toward depression. Since the Practical type is not known for having a philosophic nature, he would be at the mercy of his own melancholy.

A straight line on the hand belonging to the Psychic category would reveal greater practicality than this type normally promises, which could be interpreted favorably.

- A head line which lies straight across the palm toward the edge or percussion of the hand is considered long, because the average length stops beneath the Mount of Apollo, (Figure 37 a). Such a straight, long Head line is indicative of a person who has decided on a practical/materialistic course in his life, and knows exactly what he wants out of life and how to go about getting it. Without a fork on such a line, it gives a clue to a somewhat egotistical outlook; this person doesn't look right or left, and is only concerned with matters that relate to him. If such a Head line were to have a small fork in the direction of the Mount of

Luna, it would be an indication of imagination, yet well-disciplined. (Figure 38 b).

- The straight Head line that is shorter than the above mentioned, (Figure 37 a), but with good depth, signifies a practical disposition with common sense. Someone with this line is not side-tracked into many other avenues, but concentrates on what he does best. This Head line usually belongs to the Practical hand; it does not reflect diminished mental capacity. Rather, it shows concentrated effort, and I have observed hands with this type of Head line whose owners possess a very keen mentality. It is more important that the line be straight and without unfavorable dots or islands, which will be discussed later in this chapter.

- As mentioned above, a gently curving Head line is normal when belonging to the Psychic/Intuitive, and to a lesser degree to the Conic/Artistic types, but a line that slants excessively, ending up on the Mount of Luna itself or one that is directed toward the wrist after separating from the Life line, is abnormal in its course and reflects a somber and morbid outlook with a tendency toward suicide (Figure 37 d). This kind of formation of the Head line should be balanced by a strong thumb.

Forks on the Head Line:

Forks on this line add an extra dimension to the mentality. As already discussed, a very long and straight line will benefit from a fork toward the Mount of Luna; such a person would be more understanding of human nature. (Figure 38 b).

- A fork at the end of a long, slightly curved Head line (Figure 38 a), signifies a talent for self-expression, both verbally and in writing; this is therefore referred to as the "Writer's fork." If this is coupled with a long finger of Apollo, it is almost a certainty that such an individual has abilities for writing. People with this formation also instinctively have an understanding of human nature, and they can see both sides of a story or problem. This ability would be an asset in many professions, from the psychologist to the social worker, as well as to an actor, since he can easily put himself into the character he portrays.

- If a fork branches toward the Mount of Mercury, the sphere of "expression," it is often referred to as the "Lawyer's fork," (Figure 38 c), because this profession is associated with a facility for communication and expression.

- A three-pronged fork, (Figure 38 d), with a straight main line, one fork toward the Mount of Mercury, and the other directed to the Mount of Luna shows an individual of great versatility and keen intelligence, because he is endowed with common sense as well as creative imagination.

- A Head line that divides into two large forks at the end. (Figure 38 e) is not as favorable, because it often signifies a "torn" personality who has difficulty concentrating on any one thing. (Figure 38 f).

The Wavy Head Line: (Figure 39 a)

A line that is wavy and is also marked with changes in the depth reveals uncertainty in some area of the individual's life, and since this is called the "line of mentality," it will refer to his intellect.

Interruptions and Obstacles:

An interrupted Head line that shows an influence line "mending" it, so to speak, may reflect a trauma from an accident in the past, (Figure 39 b). The influence line is a sign of recovery, provided that the line continues smoothly.

A line that is frazzled, much interrupted with islands, (Figure 39 c and d), shows feeblemindedness, and a lack of logical thought patterns. This may be found in hands of the mentally retarded, or at best, in those whose concentration for learning is impaired. In sever cases, such a Head line would be coupled with a short or deformed thumb.

THE HEART LINE

The course of this line, (Map, C-C), reveals our emotional make-up, but the line itself, with regard to depth, color and smoothness, deals primarily with our physical health.

The Starting Points:

- The Heart line which starts on the Mount of Jupiter shows loyalty and reliability in affections. Such a person has very high standards and expectations of the ones he loves (Figure 39 a). If a line should start from the finger of Jupiter itself, it indicates that such a person could be blind to the faults in those he worships, which is bound to result in disappointments later on. (Figure 40 b)
- The Heart line starting between and below the fingers of Jupiter and Saturn reveals a deep but calm disposition as it relates to the affections, which lies somewhere between the idealism of Jupiter and the passions of Saturn. (Figure 40 c).
- When the Heart line rises from the Mount of Saturn, such a person could be passionate, but self-gratifying. His primary interest lies in his own desires and needs. (Figure 40 d). These characteristics are further enhanced if the line rises from the finger of Saturn itself. (Figure 40 e).
- If the Heart line is excessively long and covers the entire palm, (Figure 40 f), this signifies an overabundant need for affections, with a tendency toward jealousy.

The Positions of the Head Line:

The space between the Head and Heart lines is called the "Quadrangle." (Figure 40). This space is important, because through it a person reveals how he is going to deal with affairs of the heart and head, or logical reasoning. These two major lines should not infringe on each other's territories.

- If the Heart line lies low on the palm and approaches the sphere of the Head line, it suggests that such a person's private life and affections will most likely interfere with his reasoning, because the quadrangle will be narrowed, (Figure 41 a).
- If, on the other hand, the line of Head leaves its position and encroaches on the Heart line (figure 41 b), this indicates that such an individual will be heartless and calculating in getting what he wants. Such a constellation reveals a tendency toward crimes of the premeditating type. Cheiro describes such a case

in his book, "Language of The Hand," where a physician mur-
dered many of his wealthy clients after talking them into sign-
ing over their life insurance policies to him. This resulted in a
famous trial and conviction in Chicago in the 1930's. The position of the Head and Heart lines were completely normal in this
person's **LEFT** or "birth" hand, but as his greed and criminal
activities progressed, the Head line completely took over the
Heart line. (Figure 41 c).

THE SIMIAN LINE

When the lines of Heart and Head are fused together as one, it is
referred to as the "Simian line," (Figure 42 c). The joining of these two
principal lines are found in the hands of apes and monkeys. When
present in human hands, it must not automatically be taken as a sign
of low mentality.

It is of greater importance if the Simian line appears in the right
or in both hands. Such a person will pursue his goals or desires with
a dogged singlemindedness. This may work positively for the individual whose efforts and intentions are directed into creative, worthwhile endeavors. However, the lack of objectivity, which is implied by
the melting together of the two lines, can never be interpreted positively.

The Quality of the Heart Line:

In all lines, smoothness and a light pink color are an indication of
good health.

- If the Heart line has many hairline branches, it indicates
quantity rather than quality of the affections, and reveals a
flirtatious nature. But if the line is heavily frazzled, this would
be an indication of potential health problems, such as high cho-
lesterol, etc. A broad and chained Heart line rising from Saturn
reveals contempt for the opposite sex, but if pale and broad, it
signifies indifference.
- If a Heart line is bright red, it is an indication of exaggerated
passion and/or a hot temper.

- Islands, dots and frazzles on the Heart line are obstacles, which give a clue to potential or present health problems, depending on the severity. This will be discussed below under "Other Markings."

OTHER MARKINGS ON THE PALM

I have already touched upon these when describing the major lines, as they are of special significance when appearing on one of these lines. But they can also be found in other parts of the palm, such as on the various mounts and in the center of the hand. These markings could never have resulted from folding or unfolding of the hands, and are therefore a manifestation of our central nervous system. As such, they provide added features to the total evaluation of the hand.

The Island:

Islands on any of the lines, but especially on the major ones, are an unfavorable sign. They indicate weakness, and are a reflection of potential or present health problems, but if the line continues smoothly after the island, health has been restored.

On the Heart line, an island refers to physical difficulties that can affect that organ, rather than to a "broken heart" resulting from disappointments with regard to the affections. On the Head line, an island points to trauma or injury to the head or brain, revealing a lack of logical thought and concentration during the length of such an island. On the Fate line, which will be discussed in the next chapter, the island suggests temporary indecision, or a set-back in goals, (Figure 43).

Horizontal Bars:

Any horizontal markings are hindrances and/or interferences, and decrease the good qualities attributed to an otherwise favorable line. These bars are most detrimental if found on one of the major lines, but it will depend on how or if the line following the cross-bar continues.

Other horizontal markings are the "worry lines," often encountered on the Mounts of Venus and Lower Mars, (Figure 43 b). They indicate a highly sensitive disposition that is given to worrying excessively.

The Cross:

Crosses are mostly unfavorable signs. When found on a major line, they have a greater significance, and show difficulties and disappointments related to the particular area where they are encountered.

The only two places where a cross is of positive value is in the space called the "Quadrangle" between the Head and Heart lines. (Figure 43 c). This cross is called the "Mystic Cross," and those who have it possess a high degree of intuitive faculties. This is even further enhanced if found in the Psychic/Intuitive hand, coupled with long, smooth and tapered fingers.

The second location where a cross is a favorable sign is on the Mount of Jupiter (Figure 43 c), in which case it enhances the leadership abilities which are usually achieved if the finger of Jupiter is strong and straight, and of at least average length, (Figure 43 c).

Broken Lines:

They are never favorable, but if the ends are connected by an influence line, it promises recovery, (Figures 36 e, 39 b, 43 d).

Breaks in the Head line indicate a disruption of the logical thought pattern, but if an influence line connects both ends of the lines, it is a sign that normal functioning of the brain has been restored. An influence line must not be confused with a "double" Head line, which is relatively rare, where two lines running separate courses, exist. This would reveal that its owner leads two separate lives.

Squares:

A favorable marking, squares on any line are a sign of protection where they occur; (Figure 43 e). On the Head line, it reveals ingenuity and resourcefulness, and on the Life line it symbolizes protection against illnesses.

Tassels and Frayed Lines:

Any line that is frayed or ends in a tassel is a sign of weakness and diminishing energy, (Figure 43 f). On the Life line, a tassel is usually at the end near the wrist, which indicates an ebbing of the life forces. Frayed lines or "frazzles" can be found at the end or within lines, and are especially negative if present on a major line, which signifies loss of energy and strength.

Chained Formations:

These are often present at the beginning of a line, and especially at the starting point of the Life and Head lines, (Figure 43 h). This may reveal difficulties in childhood, but if the line continues smoothly afterwards, it is a sign that the difficulties have been "conquered." Most palmists agree that chained formations in the Heart line refer to the heart as an organ and not to the affections. Chained formations, as are dots and islands, are obstacles and may indicate tendencies or present physical difficulties involving the heart. If found in the Head line other than at the beginning, it reflects a loss of clear thinking, and must therefore be considered a weakness concerning the intellect.

Capillary Lines:

These are hairlines that are either ascending or descending from the main lines; the latter is less favorable. Hairlines are thinner at the ends, which is one way to check whether they are ascending or descending.

These hairlines are signs of weakness similar to the chained formations. When the entire palm is covered by a network of such spider-web lines running aimlessly in all directions, a highly nervous temperament and mental distress are indicated.

Wavy Lines:

A wavy Head line shows a lack of concentration. If found in a student's hand, it is certain that he is very easily distracted. A wavy Heart line gives a clue to a fickle disposition concerning the emotions and affections. Waviness in the Fate line, (Figure 43 j), shows a fluctuating philosophy and uncertainty in career or goals.

Dots:

Dots on any of the lines indicate temporary difficulties in the areas where they exist, (Figure 43 k).

Figure 35,
Map of the Palm

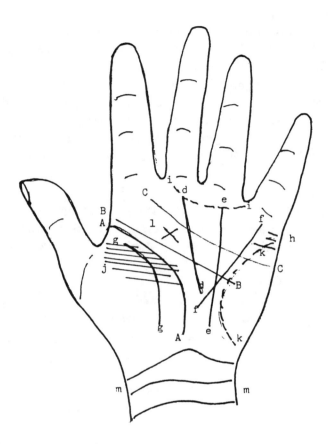

A-A	The Life Line	
B-B	The Head Line	} The Major Lines
C-C	The Heart Line	
d-d	The Fate Line	
e-e	The Apollo/Sun Line	
f-f	The Mercury/Health Line	
g-g	The Mars Line	
h-h	The Marriage/Relationship Lines	} Minor Lines and Markings
i-i	The Girdle of Venus	
j-j	The Worry Lines	
k-k	The Intuition Crescent	
l-l	The Psychic Cross	
m-m	The Bracelets (3)	

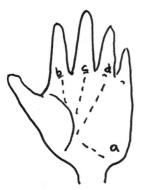

Figure 36 a-d
Forks on the Life Line

Figure 36 e
Interrupted Life Line

Figure 36 f
Life Line with
Influence Line

STARTING POINTS OF THE HEAD LINE

Figure 37 a
With Life Line

Figure 37 b
Chained to Life Line

Figure 37 c
Inside the Life Line
but Straight Course

Figure 37 d
Inside the Life Line,
Too Sloping

Figure 37 e
Separation from
the Life Line

Figure 37 f
Separation too Wide

FORKS ON THE HEAD LINE

Figure 38 a
Self Expression

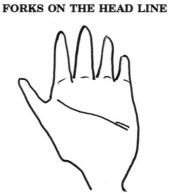

Figure 38 b
Very Long Line

Figure 38 c
Lawyer's Fork

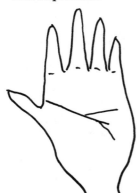

Figure 38 d
Very Keen Mentality

Figure 38 e
Forks Too Large

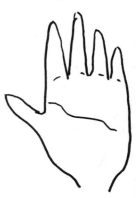

Figure 39 a
Wavy Head Line

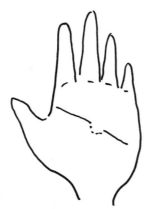

Figure 39 b
Interruption with
Influence Line

Figure 39 c
Frazzled, Interruption

Figure 39 d
Islands, Dots, etc.

THE HEART LINES STARTING POINTS

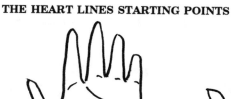

**Figure 40 a & b
From Jupiter**

**Figure 40 c
Between Jupiter
and Saturn**

**Figure 40 d & e
From Saturn
and Finger**

POSITION OF HEART LINE

**Figure 40 f
Excessive Length**

**Figure 41 a
Heart Line Too Low**

**Figure 41 b
Head Line Too High**

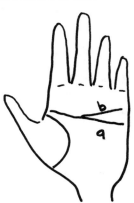

**Figure 41 c
Headline Encroaches
on Heart Line**

**Figure 42 a
Simian Line**

**Figure 42 b
Partial Simian**

**Figure 42 c
Partial Simian
Influence Line**

Figure 43,
Other Markings on the Palm

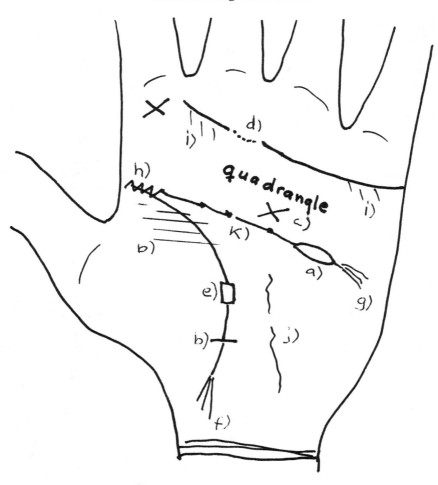

a)   An Island on Head Line
b)   Horizontal Bar on Life Line and Worry Lines on Mt of Venus
c)   The Mystic Cross in the Quadrangle, and on Mount of Jupiter
d)   Broken Line on Heart Line with Influence Line
e)   Square on Life Line
f)   Tassle at the End of Life Line
g)   Frazzled/Frayed End of Head Line
h)   Chained Life and Head Lines at the Beginning Point
i)   Capillary Lines on Heart Line
j)   Wavy Fate Line
k)   Dots on Head Line

8

The Minor Lines

THE FATE LINE

THIS IS PROBABLY THE MOST IMPORTANT OF THE MINOR LINES, MINOR ONLY because it is not a necessity, although it is of primary importance.

The line of Fate is alternately called the "Line of Destiny," and the "Line of Adaptability." I feel that the latter is well-suited, because the people possessing this line are striving to adapt their inner self to the world-at-large, and they develop a strong philosophy to achieve that goal.

According to Cheiro, it is important to observe in what type of hand the Fate line exists, the Conic and the Psychic hands than in the Square or Spatulate. The reason for this occurance is that the former types are by nature more attuned to philosophic and theoretical idealism than the other two types, whose first and foremost aim is to translate their knowledge and know-how into practical and viable endeavors, rather than into reflective or introspective philosophizing. If the line of Fate is therefore present among these two categories, it is that more worthy of notice, for it adds insight and understanding of human nature.

The closer the line comes to its destination - the Mount of Saturn - the stronger is a person's philosophy of life and his efforts toward self-actualization.

Starting and Ending Points:

- If the line starts low in the hand from or near the wrist, it indicated that the person has set goals early in life. This starting point also reveals well-developed social instincts.

- If the line continues upward into the palm and stops at the Head line, it signifies that he is not setting new goals or searching for new challenges after the age of 30 or 35. (Next Chapter, Time measured on the Hands). This individual may be completely satisfied with his career and private life and is not contemplating new directions, (Figure 44 a).

- If the line continues past the Head line, it would signify untiring efforts toward reaching for new things, (Figure 44 b).

- If the Fate line starts higher on the palm, it indicates that such a person's career or personal goals were not set early, rather, that he has "come into his own" at a later date, (Figure 44 c).

- Another starting point is from the Life line itself, (Figure 44 d). If the lines of Fate and Life are tied up, it shows a strong family influence in the early years, which may be either positive or negative.

- If the Fate line starts from the Mount of Venus itself, crosses the Life line and then follows its path toward the Mount of Saturn, or if a branch should spin off toward the Mounts of Apollo or Mercury, it could be an indication of inborn talent that runs in the family, such as in music or the arts, (Figure 44 e).

- The starting point from the Mount of Luna shows outside influence. Such a person's career or success is somewhat dependent upon people other than themselves. This formation may be seen in the hands of politicians or actors, and it can also apply to individuals who marry successful or wealthy individuals who catapult them into success by association. (Figure 44 f).

Branches Into Other Directions:

- If a branch from the Fate line veers off in the direction of the Mount of Jupiter, it signifies that a person's efforts and goals are headed toward leading or guiding others; this individual likes to be in charge of things. This will be especially enhanced by a long and strong finger of Jupiter, (Figure 45 a).

- A branch toward the Mount of Apollo indicates self-actualization and efforts in creativity; or it may be seen in the hands of someone who strives for harmony and personal happiness in his life. This will be enhanced by an Apollo finger of at least average length, (Figure 45 b).

- A branch toward the Mount of Mercury (Figure 45 c) may indicate goals and efforts in any fields, such as science, business or music. Since this sphere is associated with the art of communication and expression of any kind, and Mercury is also referred to as "the finger of enterprise," it encompasses many areas. Success in the various fields will be further enhanced by a long Mercury finger.

A Second Line of Fate or "Sisterline":

A second line that accompanies the main line during part of its course is sometimes called a "Sisterline," and is a sign of strength. But if this line should become stronger than the main line, or if its branches run to any of the above described directions, the branch line becomes the main focus in a person's life.

Other Markings:

Markings on the Fate line, as discussed in the previous chapter, such as dots, crosses, islands, bars, interruptions and waviness, with the exceptions of the square, are not favorable indications; they weaken the good qualities ascribed to the line of Fate.

It is debatable whether a Fate line with these negative markings, signifying obstacles, is more or less favorable than the absence of the line itself. Is it better to have tried and failed, or not to have tried at all? I leave this eternal question for my readers to answer.

THE APOLLO LINE

This line is also called the "Sun Line," "The Line of Brilliancy," or "The Line of Success." It has different starting points, but its destination is on or near the Mount of Apollo. As is the case with the Fate line, it is important to observe in what hand type the "Sun Line" appears, because it is more often present among the Conic/Artistic,

Philosophic or Psychic types. Whenever it makes its appearance in the Square or Spatulate hands, it takes on an even greater significance.

This line, as the various names for it imply, refers to success, brilliance, etc., but these qualities are as much an indication of a personal fulfillment, resourcefulness and adaptability, as they are a yardstick of "outer success." If this were the criterion for the "Sun Line," there would be very few people having one, but it is not an uncommon line to possess. It is further an indication of good social skills.

The Starting Points:

This line may have its inception from the Life line, the Mount of Luna, the Head or the Heart line.

- If the line starts from the Life line close to the wrist, this reveals that a person's entire life has been devoted to the arts or to the appreciation of beauty; such an individual is born with good taste. Whether a career has resulted from it is confirmed from other features: a strong branch from the Fate line toward Apollo, a curving Head line, possibly forked in the direction of the Mount of Luna, a long finger and well-developed Mount of Apollo, (Figure 46 a).
- When the Apollo line is marked in a hand with a curving Head line, success or talent is more likely to occur in the field of literature or poetry, revealing an imaginative nature.
- If the Sun line starts from the Mount of Luna, it signifies a career or interest in politics or the stage, because this starting point suggests a greater dependence on the whims or influence of others, (Figure 46 c).
- Rising from or close to the Head line, success occurs through the individual's own endeavors, but it happens later in life, (Figure 46 c).
- Starting from the Heart line, the Apollo line indicates good taste and an appreciation of all things beautiful. Such a person may come into his or her own late in life. Multiple lines show a variety of interests, but they would be too diverse to result in a successful career, (Figure 46 d).

THE MERCURY LINE

Palmists are not in total agreement with regard to the interpretation of this line, which is also referred to as the "Line of Health" or "The Hepatica." A person possessing this line does not need to rely on logic alone, for he is endowed with an inborn understanding and insight, and he is quite often "his own best doctor." If such a line is encountered in the hands of doctors or nurses, it will be very favorable, because it makes them excellent diagnosticians. The stronger the line, the greater the reliance on this unconscious "sixth sense," (Figure 47 a).

According to Cheiro, this line has its inception from the Mount of Mercury, and not from the palm as the other lines. He asserts that the absence of this line is an indication of robust health. It should never become so strong or cross the Life line, as this would prove a "fatal meeting," (Figure 47 b).

THE MARS LINE

When such a line exists on a hand, it runs parallel to the Life line on the inner side of it, (Figure 35 g-g). It is sometimes called the "Guardian Angel" line, which is supposed to protect its owner during a certain period of his life, for it may accompany the Life line for a short or long span.

Some palmists who believe in reincarnation ascribe to that line the protective influence of that person's dear departed friend or family member who watches over him from the other side.

THE GIRDLE OF VENUS

This is a semi-circular line that swings between the fingers of Jupiter and Mercury, (Figure 35 i-i). Some palmists have ascribed to the Girdle of Venus, which takes its name from the goddess of love, an overabundance of sensuality. According to Cheiro, this is an exaggerated assumption because the Mount of Venus is located in the LOWER half of the hand, which is more relative to the animal side of nature, while the Girdle of Venus is situated in the UPPER half of the hand, the mental-neocortical hemisphere. Therefore, the characteristics of the Girdle of Venus cannot be the same as those of the Mount. He asserts that people who possess this line would be more apt to dream and fantasize, or write about sexual experiences than be veritable Casanovas or Don Juans.

The Girdle of Venus suggests that people who have it are sensitive and receptive to outside stimuli, and possess a tendency toward high and low mood swings, especially if the Girdle is fragmented into little pieces. Conversely, if it is reinforced by one or more parallel lines, the desire for adventure and/or preoccupation with sex will be very strong. In this case, it would be a great advantage to have a firm thumb as a balance.

THE INTUITION CRESCENT

Some call it the "Line of Intuition." It runs in a semi-circular path from the face of the Mount of Mercury to that of the Mount of Luna, or it is found on the Mount of Luna alone, (Figure 35 k-k).

The existence of this line, or crease, is easier to observe if the hand is relaxed with the fingers bent. The Intuition Crescent must not be confused with the Mercury line, (Figure 35 f-f), even though they are both located in the same general area, and might even touch each other. The Intuition Crescent appears more frequently in the Philosophic, Conic and the Psychic hand types, but may be found in the Square or Spatulate as well. If encountered in these two latter types, it adds shrewdness and an instinctive good business sense; these people can "smell a bargain" or a good deal instantly. Wherever this line is evidenced, it reveals highly developed intuition, presentiment or clairvoyance in various degrees and a sixth sense. This gift of intuition manifests itself in vivid dream, or in the inspired usage of the spoken or written word. An orator or poet would benefit by having this Intuition Crescent, which further reflects a highly-strung, sensitive temperament.

THE MARRIAGE OR RELATIONSHIP LINES

These are horizontal markings on the Mount of Mercury, and start on the outer edge or percussion of the hand, (Figure 35 h-h).

These lines indicate the ability to enter a give-and-take relationship with someone else. The lines do not show whether it signifies marriage or a meaningful relationship, for the presence of such a line is not a "legal" sign.

A number of lines in that space reveals several relationships during the person's life, and indicates a warm and giving nature. Conversely, I have recently examined a man's hand without any such lines who has been married to the same woman, with three children, for over 30 years. I pitied his wife without knowing anything about her, because the absence of these lines confirmed my other findings in his hand, which revealed self-gratifying features. His sensuality was evident, seen in the well-developed Mounts of Venus and Luna, but the soft and flabby texture of the hand with very puffy third finger sections on the Square/Materialistic hand type revealed an excess in food, drink or sex, also showing a lack of physical endeavors.

The stronger and deeper the Marriage/Relationship lines, the greater and more lasting the influence.

- If the line exists close to the Heart line, (Figure 48 a), it signifies an early relationship, from 14-21 years.
- If the line lies approximately in the middle between the Heart line and the base of the Mercury finger, the time frame is about 21-28 years (Figure 48 b).
- If the line is situated 3.4 upwards in that space, it indicates approximately 28-35 years, etc. (Figure 48 c).
- Lines that end in a descending curve, (Figure 48 d), or those with islands, dots or bars, show a troubled relationship or separation if the line should divide in half, (Figure 48 e).

Vertical Markings:

Vertical markings on the Mount of Mercury show an interest in children, which may be an indication of parenthood, but not necessarily. It is, however, a sign of a "nurturing personality;" this could include the care of pets, animals or those weaker than oneself, (Figure 48 f).

THE BRACELETS

Usually, there are three in number. The Bracelets have little importance in the evaluation of the hand, except to confirm the general state of health of the individual.

- If the Bracelets are well-defined, clear and distinct, and lie parallel to each other, it suggests a robust and healthy constitution, (Figure 35 m-m, and Figure 49 a).
- If the first Bracelet closest to the wrist rises upward into the palm, it is a sign of a malfunction in the reproductive organs, in both men and women, (Figure 49 b).

The story goes that in the Ancient Greek Civilization, all women had to appear before the priest to have their hands examined before they were allowed to marry. If the first Bracelet closest to the wrist rose up into her hand, the priest would not give permission for the marriage for it would be a sign of either infertility or difficulties in childbearing; instead, he made the young woman a Vestal Virgin of the temple.

THE STARTING POINTS OF THE FATE LINE

Figure 44 a

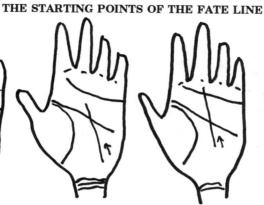

Figure 44 b   **Figure 44 c**

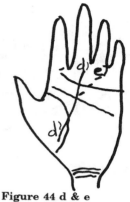

Figure 44 d & e

Figure 44 f
Starting Points
of Fate Line

Figure 45 a, b, c
Branches of Fate Line

Figure 45 d
"Sisterline" of Fate Line

Figure 46 a & b
Starting Points of Apollo Line

Figure 46 c & d

Figure 47 a & b
The Mercury Line

MARRIAGE AND RELATIONSHIP LINES

Figure 48 a, b, c

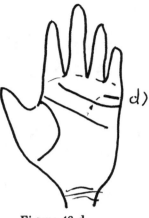

Figure 48 d

Figure 48 e

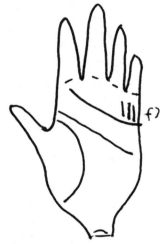

Figure 48 f
Vertical Markings

Figure 49 a

Figure 49 b

The Bracelets

9

Interpreting Time

AN APPROPRIATE TIME FRAME CAN BE ESTIMATED FROM THE LINES OF LIFE, Head and Fate, but I implore my readers to keep in mind that these measurements are hypothetical and therefore may not be accurate.

It is of utmost importance to compare both hands. If you happen to have a short Life line that does not complete the circle around the Mount of Venus, don't despair because it does not indicate that you are going to die young. A short Life line in the left hand and one of average length in the right, might show a congenital predisposition toward a certain illness, or the left hand may not have kept up with the development indicated in the right hand. Whatever the case may be, one can inherit tendencies toward a disease, but never the disease itself. If this is of great concern to you, it could give you the incentive to lead a healthy life by eating and exercising properly.

TIME ON THE LIFE LINE

A quick and easy way to get an approximate time frame is by drawing an imaginary line from the tip of the Saturn finger toward the Life line, (Figure 50). At the point of meeting the Life line, the approximate age is 35. While in many hands this indicates about the middle in the course of this line, it varies from hand to hand because of the difference in the size, and especially in the shapes of the palm.

According to Judith Hipskind's book, "Palmistry The Whole View," if both sections of the Life line before and after this meeting point are about the same length, the first half - about 35 years - and the remaining life span have equal significance, but if the length before this hypothetical intersection is shorter, a person's "35-plus-years" carry greater weight in the individual's development.

THE SYSTEM OF SEVEN

Most palmists, including Cheiro, apply the "system of seven" with regard to time and dates. From a medical and scientific standpoint, the number seven is an important marker. Gail Sheehy, in her book "Passages," used the span of seven to separate the various passages and stages we go through in our lives.

Cheiro interpreted the lines of Life and Fate together to establish an approximate time frame, for he found that these lines interrelate with each other, while he used the lines of Head and Heart as a guide or compass. As you can see in (Figure 51), the Life line is divided into sevens starting from its inception, and the Fate line is measured from the wrist section upward to the finger mounts.

- If the Fate line starts from or near the wrist, such an individual feels a strong sense of purpose early in life, (see previous chapter, Figure 35 d-d).
- If the line stops at the Head line, which indicates approximately 35 years, it signifies that its owner is not contemplating new challenges at that time.
- If the Fate line continues past the Head line and intersects with the Heart line, this point measures about 49 years, and reveals ongoing efforts toward new challenges.
- If the Fate line continues past the Heart line, (50 years), it indicates an undying search for new avenues, which will probably be this person's philosophy for his entire life, especially if the line ends at the Mount of Saturn.

THE TIME GUIDE

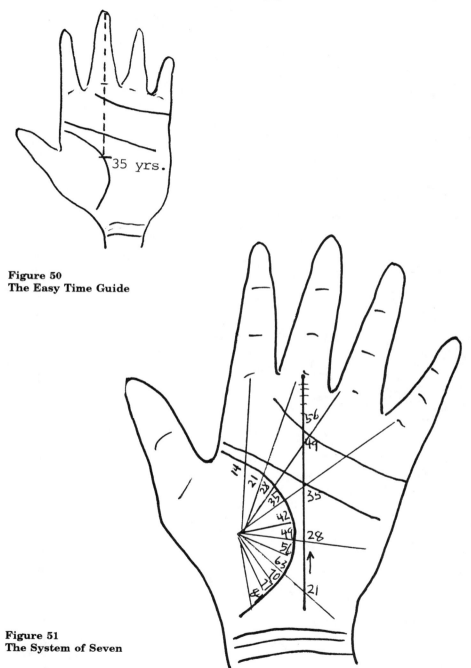

Figure 50
The Easy Time Guide

Figure 51
The System of Seven

10

Right Versus Left Hand

As STATED PREVIOUSLY, IT IS VERY IMPORTANT TO COMPARE OUR TWO HANDS. At birth, they may have looked alike with regard to shape, length of palm and finger setting, etc., but it is certain that, as we get older, the right hand becomes the dominant "tool" in right-handed people, and vice versa if left-handed.

THE BRAIN

Our brain governs our various physical movements and intellectual functioning. The Neocortex is the newer and more developed part in a person's brain, and dictates logical thinking and problem solving; it is also the seat of our ego. The Hypothalamus is situated in the "old" brain of the Limbic System, and represents our ID and inherited DNA. Messages between the old and new brain are related and transmitted through the Corpus Callosum and our central nervous system. The myriad of nerves from the brain to our hands leave their marks upon the palmar surface, and since the right hand has greater functioning, if right-handed, it reflects our impulses to a larger degree than the "birth" hand.

There may be exceptions, especially with regard to those individuals who are ambidextrous; this has to be taken into consideration when evaluating the hands. This area has not been explored, and I plan to do more research on the subject.

To illustrate the differences and changes that can take place, I am using my own hands as an example, since I can readily verify or disclaim the data observed in my own hands. Secondly, I am, chronologically speaking, of a mature age, and my central nervous system has had many years in which to register the changes. (HANDPRINT 1, Left Hand, PRINT 2, Right Hand).

RIGHT VERSUS LEFT HAND
Unchanged Characteristics:
- The Life line in both hands follows a similar course, with the starting and ending points roughly in the same place. Both Life lines possess Influence lines that travel parallel to the Life lines, which indicates resistance toward illnesses and infections, which I can readily confirm. I have been blessed with excellent health and energy, which is also revealed in the pink color of the lines.
- Both hands have a Mars line, which is evidenced on the Mount of Venus. This "Guardian Angel" line starts from the Life line at about the same point in each hand, and accompanies the Life lines during approximately the same span, (See Mars line, Figure 35 g-g).
- Not seen from the handprint is that the thumbs are firm at the base section. The "tip" phalange is more flexible and outward-bending in the right thumb.
- Also basically unchanged are the shapes of my hands and fingers, except for the length of the Jupiter finger and the position of the Apollo finger, which will be explained below.

THE CHANGES IN THE HAND AND PALMAR SURFACE
The most important change has occurred in the Head and Heart lines, which in any hand are the focal points. As you will notice, the Head line in both hands is widely separated from the Life line, which indicates an inborn spirit of independence, but on the negative side, it reveals a tendency toward impulsiveness and rashness in making decisions, which I can also attest to.

The Head Line:

You can observe a great change from the left to the right Head line. The left one is shorter and ends under the Mount of Apollo, which is considered an average length, but the waviness in its course weakens the quality and shows indecision.

Forks from the Head line are present in both hands, but they start from different points. In the left hand, the fork is beneath the finger of Saturn and continues in the direction of the Mount of Luna. (PART II, Chapter 7, Figure 38 a). Such forks are often referred to as the "Writer's fork," and I will confirm that I have always liked writing, even when it wasn't required, keeping a diary and a vast private correspondence.

In my right. hand, the Head line is considerably longer, ending under the Mount of Mercury; it also follows a much straighter course than in the left hand. The "Writer's fork" leaves the Head line at a later date, approximately below and between the fingers of Saturn and Apollo, which indicates that I started writing at a later date. This is also correct, since I resumed writing steadily in conjunction with graphology.

Forks not only indicate writing ability, they reveal a basic understanding of human nature. Such individuals can put themselves into "other people's shoes" so to speak.

The Heart Line:

Probably the greatest change in the hand took place in the constellation of the Heart and Head lines. As you will observe, the Heart line in my left hand stops beneath the finger of Saturn, and forms a partial "Simian line," the influence line connecting it to the Head line. At the point where this "near fusion" takes place, it would indicate an approximate time frame of 25 years, involving the Heart and Head lines. I must confirm that I did indeed commit an act of folly which involved my affections, making a very important decision on feelings and hunches alone without the benefit of even the most superficial investigation. I turned a deaf ear to the advice of family and friends. This boldness and impulsiveness is revealed in the wide separation of the Head and Life lines, while the lack of objectivity is evidenced in the narrowing of the space between these two major lines called the "Quadrangle" at that specific point. (Figure 34).

The Girdle of Venus:

The existence of at least a partial Girdle of Venus (Figure 35 i-i) in the left hand also indicates a desire for adventure and excitement, whereas this line does not exist in my right hand, except for small fragmented lines.

The Thumbs:

I thank my lucky stars that, with the above described constellation of the lines, I was also equipped with firm thumbs of better than average lengths on both hands, which is a very much needed compensation.

What cannot be seen from the handprints is that my left thumb is firmer at the top section than the right; the latter bends out farther, indicating greater versatility than the left thumb. Since my right hand reveals a better positioning of the Heart and Head lines, which is seen in the wide and untangled "Quadrangle," (Figure 40), the possession of a more flexible thumb is a positive feature.

The Fate Line:

The starting point of the Fate line in both hands is from the INSIDE of the Life line near the wrist, (Figure 44 d), which gives evidence of an influence or interference from the family in the early years, but the course and length of the Fate lines are different.

In the left hand, the Fate line stops before reaching the Head line, which I estimate to be around 25 to 28 years, since the intersection of the Fate and Head lines symbolizes approximately 35 years. This time-frame of 25-28 would confirm my findings described in the above section concerning the Heart line, indicating that my Neocortex and its objective reasoning took a leave of absence and let the Hypothalamus and its instincts take over.

The Fate line in my right hand continues toward the Mount of Saturn, which is the destination point. The presence of a "Sisterline" accompanying the main line from the sphere of the Heart line suggests continuous efforts and growth.

The Apollo Lines:

The left hand is void of lines in that sphere, whereas my right hand shows several lines that start from the Heart line upward to the Mount of Apollo. This suggests that I have started using my creative abilities later in life, which, coupled with the "Writer's fork" on the Head line would confirm my endeavors in that and other areas.

Further enhancing the existence of creativity is the "bulge" on the outer edge (Percussion) of my right hand, below the Mount of Mercury. This also reveals resourcefulness, a feature that is not present in my left hand.

Leaning Fingers:

When holding up both of my hands, the fingers in my left hand are all well separated, while the finger of Apollo leans toward Saturn in my right hand. This reflects an excessive need for material or emotional security. After having been made aware of this undesirable characteristic from my own hands, I am now consciously trying to keep these two fingers apart, and I am giving myself mental suggestions to that effect. An exaggerated need for emotional or material security is a defense mechanism which proves to be a hindrance to personal growth.

Length of the Jupiter Finger:

The index finger on my left hand is shorter than the one in my right hand, which indicates greater assertiveness intellectually and professionally than privately, which is absolutely true.

THE CONCLUSIONS

Concluding the comparison of my two hands, I will admit that I am pleased with the growth in personal development, especially with regard to creativity and resourcefulness. Looking back at my early life, especially the teens and early twenties, the tendencies evidenced in my left hand could have proven dangerous. The more favorable features in my right hand may have been the result of a strict but stable upbringing and social structure that was present in my youth. But I also believe that some of the positive characteristics that are revealed in my hands, such as firm and long thumbs, as well as my "fingers of philosophy" with well-developed joints - a feature I used to find unattractive - have helped me to gain insight and self-knowledge. This allowed me to acknowledge the weak areas I have to work on, and lets me "hang on" in tough situations.

LEFT HANDPRINT

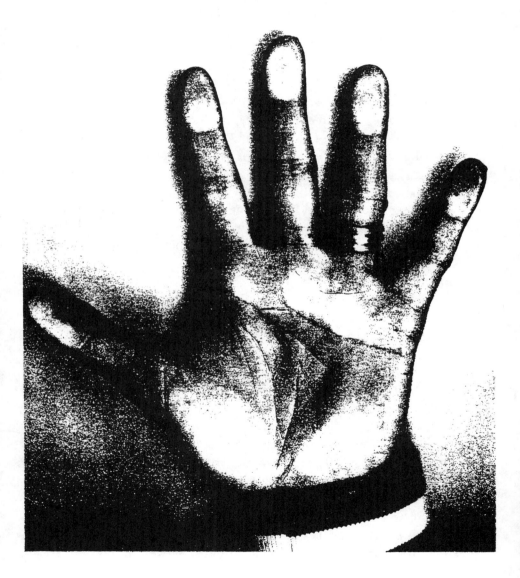

RIGHT HANDPRINT

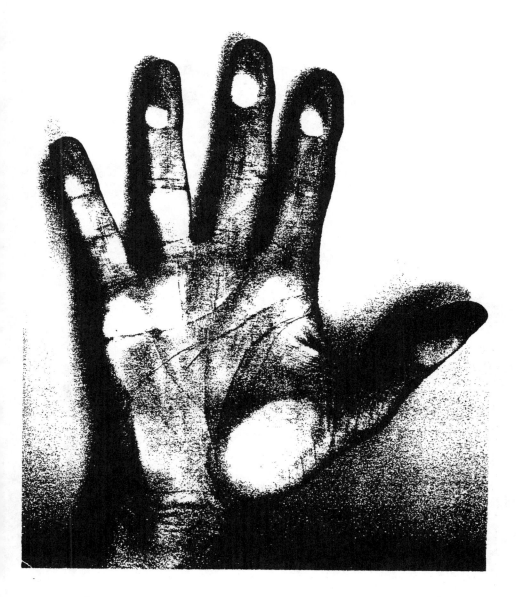

11

The Finger Patterns

THE STUDY OF THE UNCHANGING PATTERNS ON THE TOP FINGER AND THUMB sections, and on the palm itself, is a science all to its own, which is called "Dermatoglyphics." It is not the purpose of this book to make an extensive study of this science, but dermatoglyphics is of special value in medical research, and is widely studied by geneticists and criminologists because these patterns provide a great deal of information.

Although the patterns of these ridges never change, they thicken as we get older. Some palmists claim that malformations and interruptions would be an indication of impending health problems.

These linear patterns, which were formed on the epidermis, or outer layer of skin of the fetus long before birth, serve as a threefold purpose:

- they act as secretion channels for perspiration;
- as fine as they are, they provide a texture on the surface to aid gripping;
- and by forming this corrugated texture in the hand, fingers and thumb, it increases the stimulation of the nerve endings beneath the top layers of the skin, which promotes tactility.

In some people, these ridges that form the patterns are extremely thin and fine, while in others the patterns can be seen with the naked eye. It is always advisable to have a magnifying glass at hand, in order not to miss anything important when doing an analysis.

There are four basic patterns - the Loop, Whorl, Arch and Tented Arch - but among these main types exist infinite subgroupings and variations, making each print so unique that it serves as a means of identification.

The percentage of hands in which patterns of the same types appear on all fingers is very low.

THE LOOP

This pattern has two definite variations; i.e., the Ulnar and the Radial loop. (Figure 52, a and b). The combination of these two types of loops is the Composite loop, (Figure 52 c).

The Ulnar Loop:

This is the pattern most frequently found in the hands. It leads in from the percussion or outer edge of the hand. The characteristics associated with this pattern are versatility and adaptability in the face of changes that occur throughout life. There may be a tendency toward lack of firmness or stability, but this would have to be established from other findings in the hand. A good, firm thumb would provide an excellent balance to the loop pattern. People possessing mostly Ulnar loops are not confined to a narrow viewpoint.

The Radial Loop:

This loop pattern opens from the opposite side of the hand; i.e., from the thumb side. The Radial loop is found very infrequently. When present, it is encountered mostly in the thumbs and Jupiter finger. People possessing the Radial loop pattern are by nature extroverted, and like to impress themselves on the world, which may be expressed as bragging. Individuals with this pattern are more receptive to impressions from the outside world, which they absorb internally.

According to Fred Gettings in "The Book Of The Hand," the Radial loop carries similar characteristics as the whorl, and is an indication of individuality.

The Composite Loop

Another variation in the loop pattern is the Composite Loop, which is essentially a combination of the Ulnar and Radial loop, and looks similar to the letter "S". People with such Composite loops always see two distinct sides to everything, from problem solving to decision making, which is not an easy task for them. By the time they arrive at making up their minds, they may have missed opportunities. It is important to observe in which fingers, and on which hand this Composite loop appears. If found in the right hand, it has greater significance.

THE WHORL

The Whorl is an easily recognized pattern in the shape of a wheel that has a tiny knot or "peacock's eye" in the middle, with the rest of the lines concentrically twined around it, (Figure 52 d).

The Whorl pattern is not nearly as frequent as the Loop formation, and is more often found in men's than in women's hands. The Chinese palmists liken this to the "Yang/Male" and "Ying/Female" position in life. Whoever has these Whorl patterns possesses great individuality and an independent spirit. Such people often have brilliant minds, but they are of the "Type-A-personalities," which are by nature high-keyed and impatient, and are not lovers of routine work. As a result, they often suffer stomach ailments. Any artist or performer would benefit from having a whorl on the Apollo finger, which would express individuality and originality.

The Whorl pattern is the most complicated of the patterns, and, psychologically speaking, it belongs to the most complex personality type. Whorls on "favorable" hands enhance the good qualities, but in hands with many negative signs, these characteristics may be augmented.

THE LOW ARCH

This finger pattern looks like a raised bridge, (Figure 52 e). It is also called the "Simple Arch" because it is the least intricate type of pattern. It occurs in less than ten percent of all hands, and when it does make its appearance, it is more often found on the Jupiter finger in the "Earth" hand, which has few lines engraved in the palmar surface.

People possessing this Low Arch are "security-minded" for themselves and their families, but also with regard to the community at large - should they be involved in community projects. They take their commitments very seriously, and may be resentful of these "burdens," which they impose on themselves. One of the negative features of this finger pattern is stubborn defiance and lack of insight into themselves and others. Since these people have a tough time expressing their feelings of pleasure or frustration, they may explode or erupt like a volcano. Physical outlets should be as important as mental ones, for these individuals must be able to discharge hostility in a non-aggressive way.

THE TENTED ARCH

This is the least common of all patterns, and it is so called because it has an upright central core resembling a tent-pole, with the lines all draped around it, (Figure 52 f). When found, it is most likely on the index/Jupiter finger.

Like those with the Loop formation, these people's mental and emotional responses are quick. And, like the Whorl types, they are naturally high-strung and thrive on action. They possess a high degree of individuality, and often have an appreciation of the arts in many areas.

One of the byproducts of the "Tented Arch" is the idealism which these people never lose. This may not prove to be a positive characteristic, for it reflects a less than down-to-earth approach in certain given situations and problem solving, where idealism and practicality would be at odds with each other.

THE BASIC FINGER/THUMB PATTERNS
(Figure 52 a-f)

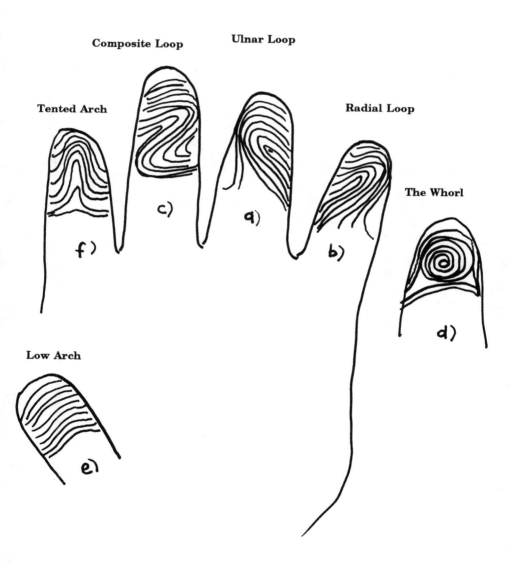

12

How To Take Handprints

THERE ARE SEVERAL METHODS FOR TAKING HANDPRINTS, FOR IT IS IMPORTANT TO have some form of recording the findings of the hands you examine for future reference, and also for research purposes. Probably the easiest method is by means of an outline and a data sheet.

THE OUTLINE OF THE HAND

Place the palm down on a sheet of paper and carefully trace around the shapes of the fingers and contours of the hand and thumb. Sometimes it is easier to take one's own outline rather than have someone else do it.

After the outline is completed on BOTH HANDS, draw in the major lines of Life, Head and Heart in the proper spaces; it is important to be very accurate, since this is the compass of the entire hand. Then continue by drawing in the minor lines as well, being precise with regard to distances, lengths of lines, etc. Continue by marking the respective finger and thumb sections, being specific about their respective length. Make note of the finger and thumb nails; their shapes can be drawn directly above or in the respective fingers and thumbs on the outline.

I always keep my magnifying glass at hand, with which I examine each finger and thumb on both hands for the finger patterns discussed in the previous chapter. In some of the hands, these skin ridges are so fine that they are barely visible, whereas in others the patterns can be seen with the naked eye. It is a good idea to note the types of pattern right above the respective fingers and thumbs on the outline, later copying this information onto the data sheet.

PRINTING WITH INK

This method of obtaining prints is and has been widely used, with apparent success. Personally, I have not had the best results from that method, either because of smearing, which distorts the pattern, or because in cases of copying a thin hand, the center of the palm does not get printed in spite of pressing down firmly on the paper. Below is a list of the materials needed for obtaining prints with this method:

- tube of water-soluble printer's ink, which is available at stores that sell graphics and artist's material;
- a 5-inch rubber roller, which is also available at those stores;
- piece of 8 x 10" (approx.) glass or plexiglass;
- stack of fairly good quality, regular-size sheets of paper without watermarks.

How To:

The printer's ink is squeezed onto the glass/plexiglass and diluted with enough water to roll out, coating the rubber roller completely. Make sure that the hand is clean and dry before doing the printing. When the palm, fingers and thumb are completely inked with the roller, leaving no spaces undone, the hand is pressed down firmly onto the sheet of paper. Gently roll it on the surface without shifting it, making sure that all parts are pressed down evenly. Remove the ink from the person's hands, first with paper towels, then with a lanolin-based hand cleaner.

PRINTS ON SMOKED PAPER

In the "olden days," palmists often used the method of prepared smoked paper for obtaining handprints.

How To:

A good quality paper without watermarks must be prepared by smoking both sides over a candle. The hand is pressed down firmly and evenly over the prepared surface of the paper. After the hand-prints are done, a fixative is used to preserve the prints and prevent smearing. Today, an acrylic fixative or even hair spray could be used for that purpose. The prints should be stored with tissue or waxed paper between them.

THE XEROX METHOD

My favorite method of recording handprints is by means of a good photo copying machine.

How To:

The hands should be placed palms down on the glass or surface of the copying machine, just as if you were copying a page of paper. If you are doing it by yourself, you must do one hand at a time, of course, but if someone else is assisting you, or vice-versa, both palms may be placed side-by-side if you select the "legal-sized" paper. Be sure to replace the cover of the machine over the hands before printing. Better results are generally obtained if the machine is set on a lighter cycle, because the lines show up darker by contrast to the lighter palm. This will depend largely on the copying machine. You must experiment until the lines are clearly visible.

HOW TO RECORD THE DATA

Your data sheet, where you record the findings in the hand, should include the following information:

1. Personal information: Name, Sex, Age of person. Date of evaluation. Right-handed, left-handed or ambidextrous.
2. Handtype. Record the main type and/or combination of types: Elementary, Square, Spatulate, Conic, Philosophic, Psychic, Mixed hand.
3. Thickness of the hand and palm: thin/soft, thin/hard, firm/elastic, thick/hard, thick/firm, or thick/soft.

4. Color of palm and lines: white, pink, red.
5. Depth of lines of Life, Head, Heart: deep, broad, clearly marked, thin.
6. Skin texture: fine, medium, coarse.
7. The length of fingers compared to the palm: long, average, short.
8. Shapes of fingers: square, spatulate, thick, thin, tapered. Note if anything is unusual: malformations, twisted.
9. Finger sections. Note which of the three sections dominates: top, middle, base.
10. The size of the thumb: short, medium, long. Note whether first or second section dominates.
11. Thumb setting: high or low, in-between.
12. Shapes of thumb: square, thick, thin, second section: "wasted".
13. Finger and thumb nails: long/broad, short/broad, short/small, conic/rounded/tapered, dish-shaped.
14. Texture of the nails: smooth, vertical/horizontal ridges, white spots.
15. Color of the nails: white, pink, bluish/gray, red, semi-circular moons.
16. Development of the Mounts. Note which ones are well-developed or flat: Jupiter, Saturn, Apollo, Mercury, Venus, Luna, Upper and Lower Mars.

PART THREE

Graphology

☆

An introduction to the science of handwriting analysis.
The history of graphology.

13

The Size of the Writing

THERE ARE FEW THINGS IN A HANDWRITING THAT ARE MORE OBVIOUS, AND HAVE a greater impact than its size. But we are often "fooled" by optical illusions; a writing may appear large if it is spread out - wider than tall - and by a generous usage of writing space, (Figure 53).

THE LARGE WRITING

The large writing usually belongs to the person who makes a large gesture, and enjoys the center stage and the limelight in one form or another. Such a writing is found among people of all walks of life, from the politician and actor to the housewife who likes to rule over her domain, which is her home and family, or the dress designer who wants the whole world to admire his designs.

The owner of a large handwriting generally enjoys the big plans and larger issues and prefers to leave the details to someone else. When one project is finished, he or she is anxious to go on to the next one, (Figure 54).

THE SMALL WRITING

This reveals excellent power of concentration. People with a smaller than average writing pay minute attention to details, and are not

easily distracted by outside influences. They show a preference toward projects rather than social contacts. Therefore, small handwritings often are found among scientists, philosophers, etc., who modestly
cast aside their own personal gains in favor of their life's work, which
is also encountered in hands of individuals doing research. Two such
examples are the writings of Mahatma Ghandi and Albert Einstein,
(Figures 55 and 56).

THE THREE ZONES IN WRITING

The total size of a handwriting is measured from the top of the
upper lengths to the lowest part of the lower zonal loops or extensions.

The handwriting is divided into three zones; i.e., the upper, middle
and lower zones. Capital letters, t-crossings, and i-dots are in the
upper zone; lowercase letters are in the "m" zone, and loops, or mere
extensions of the "y's" or "g's," are in the lower zone. The letter "f" is
the only one that encompasses all three zones, (Figure 57).
How these three zones relate to one another is very significant. Both
small and large handwritings may have one or two zones overempha-
sized.

- A large middle zone and short upper zone belongs to someone
who lives from day-to-day without any specific or definite goals;
such a person is often quite self-satisfied, (Figure 58).
- A large middle zone with a short upper, but very long and full
lower zonal loops indicates strong physical, material and/or sensual needs, neglecting the intellectual sphere, (Figure 59).
- A large middle zone with equally long upper and lower zone
extensions gives a clue that such a person knows how to materialize his or her dreams and goals. If well-balanced, the handwriting is an indication of vitality and energy, and also a bid for
attention and accolades, (Figure 60).
- An average size middle zone with balanced upper and lower
zones - which are generally longer than the middle zone - reflects a well-rounded and well-organized individual who has the
ability to materialize goals, but they will be of a different nature
than those who belong to the large, showy writing, (Figure 61).

- A small middle zone with a balanced upper and lower zone shows excellent powers of concentration and staying power in work, which is of primary importance to the individual. Such a person displays a modest and unpretentious facade, yet he is eminently self-reliant, for he does not depend on the opinions and attentions of other people as much as the individual with a large writing, (Figure 62).

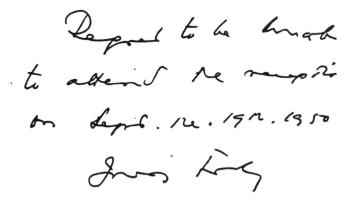

Figure 53, Handwriting Wider Than Tall

Figure 54, Very Large Handwriting/Space

Figure 55, Mahatma Ghandi

Figure 56, Albert Einstein

Figure 57, Three Zones in Handwriting

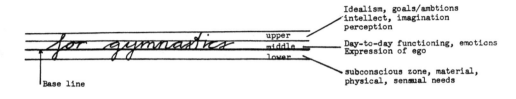

Idealism, goals/ambtions
intellect, imagination
perception

Day-to-day functioning, emotions
Expression of ego

subconscious zone, material,
physical, sensual needs

upper
middle
lower

Base line

Figure 58, Large Middle Zone - Short Upper Zone

Finished, see ya, I'm
out of here. Bye!!!
I'm so happy.

Figure 59, Large Middle Zone, Short Upper and Long/Full Lower Zone

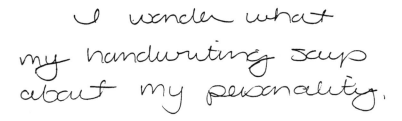

Figure 60, Large Writing, Fullness and Width in All Three Zones

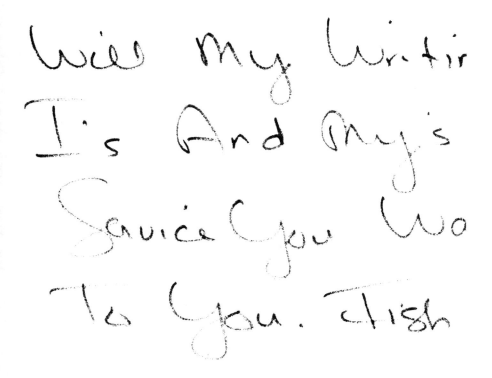

Figure 61, Average Middle Zone with Balanced Upper and Lower Zones

Graduating today was a really
emotional experience. The
hightest moment was when
Scott Necome got the award

Figure 62, Small Middle Zone with Balanced Upper and Lower Zones

This is not a personal matter,
but, would like to share this with you.
It is a great feeling to be a Graduate.

Sincerly,

14

Full and Narrow Writing

FULLNESS

A HANDWRITING IS CONSIDERED "FULL" WHEN ITS MOVEMENTS COVER A LARGER surface than average. When the opposite takes place, it is referred to as narrow or meager writing.

Generally speaking, fullness stands for enjoyment of life, sociability and generosity. Narrowness is an indication of repressed feelings, inhibitions and over-control. It is rare that a handwriting is equally full or narrow in all three zones. Imaginative people (upper zone) may be lacking in feelings or empathy (middle zone), and affectionate ones (lower zone) may not possess imagination or ambition. An abstract-thinking intellectual could also have strong erotic fantasies, which would be indicated by elaboration in the lower zone and meagerness in the middle sphere. The zonal distribution is, therefore, important in the evaluation of a handwriting.

There are cases where the lower zone is shortened or damaged by repression or illness, but is compensated for by fullness and richness in the middle and upper zones. This would indicate that this person had found a way to compensate for his lack of fulfillment in the sensual area by enriching his intellect.

Expansive movements and curvatures, such as grandiose loops and covering strokes, give the illusion of fullness, while the structure of the "m" zone may be constricted. This reveals that the writer wants

115

to give an impression of largesse and generosity, which is only a superficial veneer.

Fullness in the Upper Zone:

This is an expression of joy and cheerfulness; if these loops and
movements are executed with a flair of originality, it indicates unusual
visual and spatial perception, such as demonstrated by the signature
of famous architect Frank Lloyd Wright, (Figure 63).

If fullness in this zone is greatly exaggerated, it reflects vanity; in
extreme cases, it is a sign of "delusions of grandeur" and expresses the
inability to be realistic, (Figure 64).

Fullness in the Middle Zone:

It is in this zone that we give evidence not only of the quality and
quantity of our feelings, but the "modus operandi" of our daily functioning. Because the "m-zone" is the sphere where we express our ego,
it is important to observe each characteristic, its fullness or lack of it,
height or width, and especially how it relates to the upper and lower
zones.

A full and rhythmic middle zone reflects a harmonious and con-
tented disposition, (Figure 65), but if this zone is exaggerated in width
or length, coupled with a stunted upper zone, this indicates a lack of
intellectual interest or goals. Such a person is quite often self-centered
or self-indulgent, and does not see the need for self-improvement, (Figure 66 a).

Fullness in the Lower Zone:

Fullness in this zone is produced by either open or closed loop
formations. Incomplete loops do not finish their course and return to
the base line, which reveals unfulfilled desires or erotic fantasies. If
fullness in this zone is accompanied by heavy pressure in the writing
- the physical or psychic pressure exercised on the writing surface - it
indicates vital energy that may be expressed in healthy physical and
sexual activity; it can also indicate eccentricity or vulgarity in that
area, (Figure 66 a-h, various loops).

NARROWNESS - MEAGERNESS

Narrowness must not be confused with simplification of letter formations, which has a positive interpretation. A narrow or constricted writing speaks of want of feelings, or coldness of heart, independent of education or social standing. It is simply an expression of an uncharitable, or even inhumane nature, especially if found in the middle zone. But as fullness is not often seen in all three zones, neither is narrowness, and each zone must therefore be interpreted separately.

Narrowness in the Upper Zone:

This shows an increased capacity for abstract thinking, and it is usually produced by the omission of loops. With good upper zonal length it is a reflection of a probing and analytical mind that is essential to certain professions such as engineering, accounting, etc., (Figure 68).

Narrowness in the Middle Zone:

We speak of narrow writing if the distance between the downstrokes of the middle zone is smaller than the length of each letter, which is referred to as the "primary width," (Figure 69).

- If the letters themselves, such as "m's" or "n's," are narrow and compressed, but the distance or connection between two or more letters is wider than between one letter, it is called "secondary width." This gives an appearance of a wider, fuller writing, revealing the conscious or unconscious intention of the writer to appear less inhibited or repressed, (Figure 70).
- The form of connection most often used with a narrow writing is the "angle," which will be further discussed in Chapter 16. I mention it here to point out that the angular connection expresses feelings of frustration, inhibition and hostility, which result from inner conflicts. On the positive side, the angle also expresses precision and exactness of work habits.
- An extreme form of narrowness is the "covering stroke," in which two downstrokes cover each other. This is a reflection of severe inhibition or insincerity, (Figure 71). These covering strokes also may be found in a large writing, in which case it is less from inhibition than from a desire to bluff or cover up ineptitudes.

- Narrow writing, if coupled with an even base line and regularity, indicates considerable self-control; such a person's vital energies are often spent in self-discipline, leaving less time for enjoyment, in order to control his or her feelings. Therefore, a narrow writing always signifies a lack of spontaneity, (Figure 72).

Narrowness in the Lower Zone

Narrowness in this zone is shown either by omission or compression of the loops.

- Loops that are omitted in final letters such as "g's" or "y's" are an expression of concentration and good judgment. If applied with pressure, it signifies intensity, (Figure 73). However, if these loops are omitted in the middle of a word, it is the result of an interruption of thought and action, and must be taken as a sign of hesitancy or uncertainty, since it would be more expedient to complete the loop and bring it up to the base line to form the connection with the next letter than to interrupt the flow with a mere downstroke, (Figure 74).
- Compressed loops are indicative of unconscious frustration or inhibition. Such a person will most likely have a tense and critical disposition, and have difficulties in finding genuine enjoyment in life, (Figure 74).

SIMPLIFICATION VERSUS EMBELLISHMENT

Simplification in writing is the omission of "unnecessary" movements, such as "lead-in" strokes to capital and lowercase letters, which were part of all teaching methods. A simplified writing is a positive feature. It does not endanger the clarity and legibility, nor does it slow down the speed of writing. On the contrary, simplification usually increases the speed and expediency.

Printed capital letters followed by script show good taste and are a sign of culture; they reveal a preference for an "uncluttered" style of clothing and furnishings over frills and/or gaudy ornamentation.

Simplification shows the intelligence of the writer, since he has the ability to strip away non-essentials and zero in on the heart of the matter, (Figure 75).

Simplified writing is positive as long as it does not lead to "neglect;" over-simplification often shows a lack of legibility, and may therefore suggest sloppiness and a disintegration of good qualities, (Figure 76).

EMBELLISHMENTS

Any additional letter formations that are not called for in the various penmanship methods are considered elaborations or embellishments. They are often more an expression of pomp and vanity than an extension of fullness. A writing with wild flourishes, (Figure 77), reveals the writer's illusions and delusions. While simplification expresses the ability to "weed-out" non-essential matter, a person whose writing is embellished is often stuck on petty details, and may miss the focal points of discussions or tasks entirely, like one who cannot see the forest for the trees.

REVIEW OF CHARACTERISTICS

Fullness in upper zone	Imagination, perception, optimism.
Fullness in middle zone	Inner wealth of feelings, love of life, affection, empathy.
Fullness in lower zone	Vital physical energy, healthy sexual appetite.
Exaggerated fullness in upper zone	Ostentation, loss of reality, delusions.
Exaggerated fullness in middle zone	Self-indulgence, self-satisfaction.
Exaggerated fullness in lower zone	Erotic fantasy, eccentricity, exaggerated need of emotional and/or material security.
Narrowness in upper zone	Capacity for abstract thinking.
Narrowness in middle zone	Lack of feelings and empathy, concentration on subject matter, inhibition, repression, over-control.
Narrowness in lower zone	Inability to communicate feelings if loops do not return to base line, lack of enjoyment in life, critical and tense disposition.
Narrowness in lower zone with pressure	Intensity and concentration.
Simplification in upper and middle zone	Ability for abstract thinking; able to get to the core of the matter, good taste and sign of culture, self-reliance.
Simplification in lower zone with loops omitted at the end or word	Good judgment, concentration.
Neglected slow writing	Tendency to be evasive.
Neglected fast writing	Nervousness, insecurity, sloppiness.
Embellishments with originality	Fantasy, originality, creativity.
Exaggeration of embellishments	Fussiness about petty details, ostentation; desire for frills and pomp; Missing important matters.

Figure 66 a-h, The Lower Zone Loops

a Earthy loops, materialistic physical appetites, sensuality.

b Ineffectual loops. Sign of lack of energy, illness. Repressed sexual energy.

c Rightward-turning stroke. Altruism. Indicates simplification; expediency.

d Unyielding and aggressive. When these triangular loops interfere with the lines below: confusion and self-centeredness.

e All tie-strokes signify persistence. In lower zone they indicate a compulsive persistence. Eccentricity.

f Clannishness. It also shows a need to "hang-on" to things, especially if the leftward stroke neds in a hook.

g These rolled-in finals in loop formations show eccentricity and a peculiarity in the sexual sphere. Such people have difficulty to communicate intimately.

h Ommision of loops in a word ending in "g" or "y" shows good judgment; intensity, if with pressure in writing.

More than three different kinds of loop formation in one handwriting indicates uncertainty and possible difficulties with intimate relationships.

Figure 63, Signature of Frank Lloyd Wright

Figure 64, Exaggerated Fullness - Encrollments

Figure 65, Full and Rhythmic Middle Zone

I'm so excited for my Mary seminar. Graduation was n I've made it. Vanderbilt hi

Figure 67, Narrowness in Upper Zone

I like to fry eggs griddle every day.

Figure 68, Narrow "Primary Width"

Mr. or Mrs. Norman Dinstein
8005 Cypress Grove Lane
Cabin John, Md. 20818

**Figure 69, Primary Width Narrow,
Secondary Width Wide**

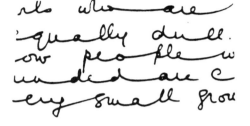

Figure 70, Covering Stroke Inhibition

when she is in washington.

Thanks Again

Figure 71. Covering Stroke, Desire to Bluff

Jeackie   Connelt

not beleefor   Groek

Figure 72, Omission of "g" Loop as Final Stroke

The regular monthly

Figure 73, Ommission of "g" Loop Within Word

my car is stuck
inside the garage

Figure 74, Compressed Lower Zone

the copies of your article
i am so glad to have
them, and shall read

Figure 75, Genuine Simplification

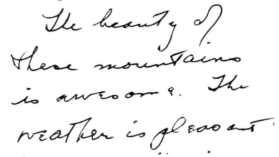

The beauty of
these mountains
is awesome. The
weather is pleasant

Figure 76, Neglected Writing, Illegible

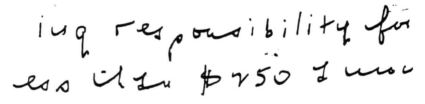

ing responsibility for
ess than $750 I was

Figure 77, Embellishments; Wild Flourishes

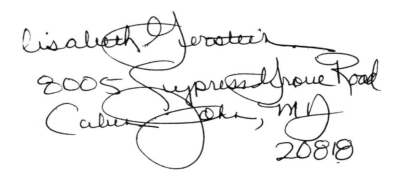

15

The Different Slants

It is very important to establish if someone is right or left-handed, because a left-handed individual often produces a steeper slant than the right-handed, especially if he turns the page sideways. The slant of handwriting is the angle that the downstrokes produce in relation to the real or imaginary writing line of the lowercase and upper zonal letters.

The slants express a whole range of emotions, from uninhibited impulsiveness, which is produced by either a far right or far left slant, to exaggerated self-control. Contributing factors will have to determine which is applicable. Klara Roman, in her book, "Handwriting - A Key To Personality," also divides the slants into three major attitudes: Compliance, Self-Reliance and Defiance, producing the right, vertical and left slant respectively. Figure 78 shows the range of slant.

THE RIGHT SLANT

This is the incline taught in all school systems. It reflects the movement to the right which, graphologically speaking, symbolizes the future and the father figure. This slant is and should be found among leaders in all professions from teachers to politicians, because it expresses a desire for communication and an interest in people and/or the world-at-large. (See figures 54, 56, 65). Generally, the right slant

125

is a sign of extroversion, but I must caution again that any single finding in handwriting must be confirmed by other correlating characteristics; we as human beings are complex and often contradictory, which results in diametrically opposed traits.

A far right slant is primarily an indication of diminished self-control and of unchecked emotional release. An even base line coupled with an extreme right slant lends stability and self-discipline to the individual. (See Figure 67).

THE VERTICAL SLANT

People who chose a vertical slant are generally endowed with poise. They have a natural and uninhibited way of expressing themselves, but they possess a built-in valve to stem the flow of their emotions. For example, it is almost a national trait of the British and French people to use the vertical slant. In countries, whose governments and policies have imposed a certain reserve of long-standing, it seems to have inhibited the unchecked emotional release in its citizens, which is also evidenced in handwriting.

Also, people of Latin origin quite often write with a right-ward slant that reveals their natural bent toward exuberance and self-expression. Below are two samples of extroverted individuals. The sample of Figure 79 is that of a British female. Figure 80 is the writing of Italian singer/entertainer Enrico Caruso.

THE LEFT SLANT

This is the opposite of the right slant, which indicates spontaneity. The left slant reflects a back-to-self attitude in some areas. Again, this is a very complex issue, since people who adopt this slant can be just as sociable and future-oriented as the right-slanted, but their ego has built-in self-protective defenses around the SELF to keep it from getting hurt.

In most cases, the slant of writing is established in young adulthood or even in adolescence. A young child who has had a poor home environment or has experienced difficulties in growing up may select a left slant, which is quite often the result of rebellion, (Figure 81).

People who have suffered disappointments and set-backs in their lives in financial, sexual or social areas may unconsciously revert from a right or vertical to a left slant. This may be of temporary duration, as in a case of loss of a loved one. When a person finds new avenues and joys in life, the slant of writing will automatically return to his or her natural movement.

THE FAR LEFT SLANT

The characteristics mentioned above are exaggerated in people using a far left slant. The handwriting expert Alfred Mendel, in his book, "Personality In Handwriting," established that in all cases of extreme left slant, individuals had unhappy childhoods. This includes such famous people as G.B. Shaw, Maxim Gorki, Henrick Ibsen and Leonardo da Vinci. The self-protective defenses built up by their ego are reflected in the attitudes. Such people always consider themselves the primary object; while they may appear extremely sociable and charitable, they may have a conscious or unconscious self-serving interest at heart. These individuals have a tendency to be cautious and suspicious, which is the result of former injuries or damage to their ego. Therefore, as mentioned before, the movement to the left symbolizes the SELF, the MOTHER and the PAST, (Figure 82).

THE MIXED OR CHANGING SLANT

Writing that changes direction within words, or within the writing, is referred to as the "mixed slant." (Figure 83). This indicates a conflict in the personality, and is an expression of indecision about everyday matters, especially if the middle zone is involved. Such an individual is see-sawing between impulsiveness and self-control. It also reflects indecision and/or changes in attitudes that may fluctuate within a short period of time. Quite often this is a sign of unreliability and volatility.

- If a capital letter, or more importantly the "personal pronoun I" (PPI, for short), is inclined more to the left in a left-slanted writing, or is more right-slanted in a right-ward leaning script,

it signifies that the person starts out impulsively, but soon re-
gains his self-discipline.

- If the beginning letter or PPI stands vertically and the rest of
the writing leans to the right or left, the individual overcomes
his initial shyness and reserve and behaves more naturally and
spontaneously, (Figure 84).

- If the last stroke of a letter is blunt; i.e., without final movement to the right, or if the final stroke turns left-ward, the writer
shuts off communication with the YOU, which can be an expression of inhibition, suspicion or cautiousness. The sample in Figure 85 shows blunt ending strokes in "m" and "n," and two left-
ward "t"-crossings.

MIRROR WRITING

A writing in which the directions of the letters are reversed, and
which is written from right to left is called mirror-writing because it
appears normal and legible when reflected in the mirror.

Such a writing can only be produced by a left-handed or ambidextrous person. An excellent example of mirror-writing is that of Leonardo
da Vinci, who was ambidextrous, and equally adept with both hands.
It is interesting that he employed a conventional right-handed style
for general communication, but used the mirror-writing in his diary,
obviously intended as a protection to keep its contents secret. (Figure
86).

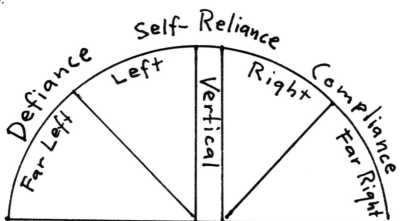

Figure 78, The Range of Slants

Figure 79, Extroverted British Female

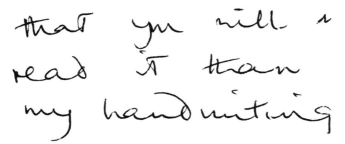

Figure 80, Writing of Italian Singer/Entertainer Enrico Caruso

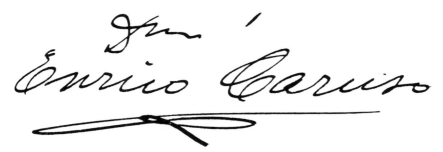

Figure 81, Female Fullness in All Three Zones

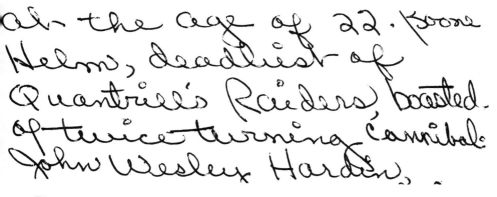

Figure 82, Far Left Slanted Narrow Writing

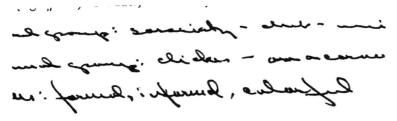

Figure 83, Mixed and Changing Slant

Figure 84, PPI Stands Vertically, Following Letters Rightward

I'm so glad high
Beach week will
I'll miss my gi

Figure 85, Blunt Finals in "M" and "N" Two Final "T" Crossings Leftward

Figure 86, Mirror Writing (Leonardo da Vinci)

16

The Way We Connect Our Letters

THE DIFFERENT FORMS BY WHICH WE CONNECT OUR LETTERS TO EACH OTHER reveals our social attitudes and much more. It not only gives a clue to our adaptability in life's situations, but it expresses our inner balance and harmony, or the lack of it. Dr. Ludwig Klages, the German psychologist and father of modern graphology, stated that "Everything Lies In The Connections."

The standard school form of the Latin alphabet provides mostly curves as connective strokes, whereas the German or Gothic forms employ primarily angles mixed with curves. The curve which we call the "garland" permits an uninhibited, smooth flow of the writing movement, while the angle requires a change of direction which briefly stems the continuity of the writing. The garland is, therefore, a faster, more expedient form of connection than the angle. It is, by nature, more spontaneous. Between these two opposite styles of connections lies the "arcade." The "thread" is a combination of the garland and the arcade, sometimes referred to as the "double curve." If completely flattened or stretched out, it is referred to as "thready writing." Figure 87 a-d shows these four basic forms of connections.

THE GARLAND

The garland connects the downstrokes of the letters with each other at the base line in a flowing movement; by virtue of its openness at the top of the letter, it symbolizes receptiveness to impressions received from the outside world.

A garland writer proceeds with a natural rhythm, without friction, reflecting a personality that seeks to avoid friction and confrontation. This avoidance of struggle has different interpretations:

- If the garland is pressed down low toward the base line, the positive features ascribed to the garland are reduced, for such a person shows a lack of resistance and enterprise, (Figure 88). If the garland is "dragged down" below the base line, it indicates pessimism and even depression, which is the opposite of what the genuine garland stands for.

- A garland writing that has pointed tips on "m"s and "n"s, etc., shows a keen mental perception and analytical abilities. Such people learn new things very quickly. (Figure 89). A garland writing with medium pressure also indicates a potential for a good memory.

The sample writing in Figure 89 is that of an 18 year old female, high school graduate. She is not only intelligent, but possesses a friendly and outgoing personality, who is willing to please. Although she still conforms to a degree to the values and environmental patterns of her childhood, seen in her adherence to the taught "Palmer method" style of letter formations, she has also started to simplify by omitting lead-in strokes to beginning letters; this indicates that she is thinking independently. Her clear and rhythmic script gives evidence of a harmonious nature, and the excellent word and line spacing reveals objective reasoning. These characteristics, coupled with her interest in people and good communication skills, would be excellent attributes in careers such as teaching, social work, public relations, etc.

THE ARCADE

This stroke is the "upside-down" garland, resembling a tent or cover, which is closed at the top.

Roman architecture provides a classic illustration of the arcade with its arches and archways. There are many different kinds of arcades. The "m"s and "n"s, for instance, are arcaded in many standard forms of writing, but the adult writer of arcades is generally not much interested in accepting new impressions from the outside world. He draws his strength from tradition and from his origins. (Figure 90). Appearances, in an aesthetic or moral sense, are often more important than the heart of the matter. Arcade handwriting belongs to all kinds of people in all types of professions; they range from the genius in art and architecture, (see Figure 63 - signature of Frank Lloyd Wright), to the ambitious bureaucrat who wishes to imitate the stature of his superiors.

While the writer of garlands may be slowed down in his activities by the impressions he receives from the life around him, the writer of arcades concentrates on his goals and proceeds with a minimum of interruptions. Such concentration can be evaluated as a positive characteristic, for his singlemindedness often leads to success in his or her endeavors.

- If the arcade appears at the beginning of the word, especially in capital letters, a certain reserve or a desire to impress exists. (Figure 91).
- The left-ward tending final arcade represents a moment of inhibition or caution. The writer instinctively holds back either feelings or warmth, when he should reach out and approach the YOU. The reasons for this may be quite different. Such a backward final arcade represents a self-protective gesture in embarrassing situations, or wishing to keep something from others, probably due to events in his past. (see Figure 85).

The Double Curve:

This is the combination of the garland and the arcade. In fast writing, it appears almost as a thread. Such wavy movement destroys the solid character of the word structure. This form of connection combines the genuine adaptability with the pretended one. The writer wishes to adapt himself at any cost. It is found in the handwritings of diplomats and psychologists, as well as in that of crooks and swindlers. It is up to the handwriting analyst to separate the two.

- If the double curve is found in fast writing, indicated by good rhythm and smooth strokes, and is still legible, the interpretation is more favorable. (Figure 92).
- If the writing has deteriorated into an illegible scrawl, often coupled with an uneven base line and many irregularities in letter formations, change of slant, etc., the double curve must be interpreted negatively. (Figure 93).

THE ANGLE

The angle-writer shows an inclination toward constant and abrupt change of directions, which is a reflection of a personality that looks for conflicts rather than avoiding them. Such an attitude is the outer manifestation of a person's inner conflicts, and it expresses either his refusal or inability to adapt to life's situations. The angle may not be present equally in all three zones of the writing.

- If found in the upper zone in capital letters and PPI (personal pronoun I) the angle reflects an ambitious drive. (Figure 94).
- An angle in the middle zone signifies a lack of feelings and consideration for others; it is often a sign of stark egotism. (Figure 95).
- Angular lower zone loops indicate an unyielding, critical and often brutal nature. (See Figure 66 d).
- Angular formations and connections in all three zones are intensified by heavy pressure in the writing, exemplified by Figure 95, which is the signature of the notorious sadist Julius Streicher. He started his career as teacher, but degenerated into a brutal criminal.

The Shark's Tooth:

This is another form of the angle, (Figure 96), which may appear either in the upper zone or on the base of the middle zone.

The Shark's Tooth, which takes the form of an inverted "v", is a more sophisticated form of aggression that may be camouflaged by superficial courtesy, but because it is not as obviously marked as the blatant forms, it is much more cutting. Figure 96 shows the shark's tooth in the middle zone in "m" and "n"s as well as in the capital "M" in "Mother."

THE THREAD

There are two variations of the thread connective, one with and the other without writing pressure in the writing.

- Where the thread is encountered within the word and without pressure, it is often a sign of lability, hysteria and neuroses, especially if coupled with an uneven base line, severe irregularities to slant, and letter formations. (Figure 97).
- The thread connection with pressure is an indication of diplomacy and fast thinking. If the writing is still legible, with an even base line, the interpretation of the thread can be evaluated favorably, but if the script is entirely indecipherable, it reveals various degrees of evasiveness and insincerity. (Figure 98).

MIXED CONNECTIONS

A mature adult's writing should show a mixture of connections. A person who uses garlands exclusively will be too receptive to outside stimuli, while those with arcades would shut themselves off from the world. The writer of angles in all three zones and throughout the entire writing would be impossible to deal with, and should be "put in chains," whereas the "thready" individual wouldn't let anyone know what he or she was thinking or doing.

The writing sample of Figure 99 is that of Adlai Ewing Stevenson who was the Democratic nominee for president of the United States in 1952 and 1956, but who was defeated by "Ike" Eisenhower both times. Stevenson's writing is of the highest intellectual quality and intelligence, but it does not show personal magnetism to appeal to the masses. The lower zone in his writing is rather ineffectual and stunted, showing a neglect in the physical/sensual sphere, which is an indication that all of his energies were spent intellectually.

Figure 100 is the handwriting of a very mature and sophisticated 18 year old youth. It demonstrates a variety of elegant and smooth connections in many letter formations as described in Chapter 2. This, coupled with excellent word and line spacing, showing his objectivity and clear thinking, indicates a high degree of intelligence and ingenuity in a colorful personality, revealed in the originality of his signature.

Figure 87 a-d, The Four Basic Forms of Connections

a)   The Garland ......*uu*......*done*.....

b)   The Arcade ...*mm*........*none*.....

c)   The Angle ...*uu*........*none*....

d)   The Thread ...——........*done*...

Figure 88, Pressed-Down Garland

caused you— Apparently the fabric was out, was reordered arrived late and was no properly treated and was

Figure 89, Garland Writing with Pointed "M" and "N"s Analytical Thinking

for so long, just waiting til it was finally here. Now at this day has arrived, I id that I feel almost sad stead of excited and jubilant

Figure 90, Arcade Writing

"Round-the-Corner Art Gallery" cordially extends to you this invitation to attend a special premier showing of the mystical crea-

Figure 91, Beginning Arcade in Capital Letter

My Many.

Figure 92, Double-Curve, Fast and Legible Writing

great day! Finally - we're
! I wonder what my
says about me ...
I'll be going to Virginia
i be great! I can't wait

Figure 93, Double-Curve, Irregularities

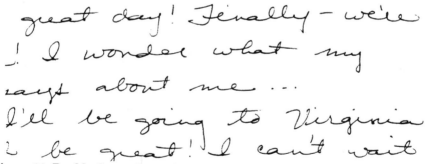

July 18, 88
should I tell you
the story about me

Figure 94, Angular Upper Zone

Figure 95, Angularity in Middle and Lower Zones

Figure 96, Shark's Tooth in Upper and Middle Zones

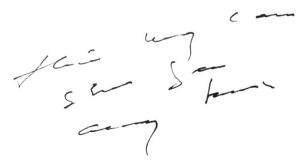

Figure 97, Thread WITHOUT Pressure, Illegible Writing

Figure 98, Thread Writing WITH Pressure

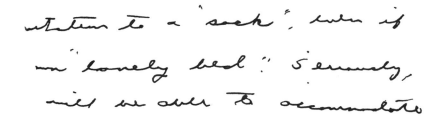

Figure 99, Mixed Connections. Writing of Adlai Stevenson

Figure 100, Mixed Connections. Writing of 18 Year Old

17

Connected Versus Unconnected Writing

CONNECTED WRITING

MOST ADULTS USE ONE OR SEVERAL FORMS OF CONNECTIONS MENTIONED IN THE previous chapter; i.e., garlands, arcades, angles or thread, or a mixture thereof. Connecting single letters into a "cursive" form of writing is taught to children in elementary schools. Later on, the writings of people reflect their individuality in style, forms and degrees of connectedness. When five or more letters in a word are "strung" together without an interruption, it is considered a high degree of connectedness; when fewer than that number are connected without lifting the pen off the paper, we call it "disconnected" writing.

A high degree of connectedness indicates a writer's logical train of thought, as well as adaptability to his environment, once again taking many other factors into consideration. (Figures 95 and 96).

Exaggerated Connectedness:

If writing shows extreme connectedness, where two or three words, or even entire lines, are linked without interruptions, it impairs the legibility unless the writer is clever enough to mark the end of the word with an elongated connecting stroke. This does not show an increased capacity for logical thinking. Such a person has a conscious or unconscious desire to appear original, while he gives away his tendency toward laziness, as the pen does not have to be moved from the writing surface. (Figure 69).

141

Connecting the "I Dots and "T" Crossings:

When "i"-dots and/or "t"-crossings are connected either backwards or with the following letter, it reveals a memory for associations. (Figure 101). Quite often it also indicates ingenuity, and is the mark of a strategist. Figure 102 exemplifies this, since the signature is that of a retired general. Such elegantly executed connections and combinations are found in the scripts or writers, artists, lawyers, psychologists and detectives. If seen in the writing of a medical doctor, it is a sure sign of an excellent diagnostician.

Connected Writing with Disconnected Capital Letters:

When the first letter, which is usually a capital or PPI, (personal pronoun I) stands by itself, while the rest of the word is connected, this suggests a brief pause between "thinking and doing," which is a positive characteristic at the "bridge" as well as at the "conference" table. (Figures 61 and 103).

Letters Connected to the Right Instead of the Left:

Lower zone loops that turn to the right without first turning to the left, as the writing methods prescribe, are a form of simplification, (Chapter 14). This is always a sign of intelligence and expediency. (Figure 100).

THE UNCONNECTED WRITING

When fewer than four or five letters in a word are connected, one speaks of an "unconnected" or "disconnected" writing.

The positive side of a disconnected writing is the gift of intuition, for the brain allows creative ideas to stop the continuity of the writing for a fraction of a second. The presence of these interruptions does not impair or disturb the movement or the rhythm of the writing, nor does it indicate an absence of logic unless there are indications to the contrary. It is not surprising that many inventors, explorers, artists, psychologists, etc., have a lesser connected writing. (Figure 104 - Famous 18th Century Spanish painter Goya).

The interpretation of a disconnected writing becomes negative if the breaks occur inappropriately and result in gaps, (Figure 105), or if the writing is illegible and appears "chopped-up," consisting mainly of downstrokes rather than up-and-downstrokes. This suggests a disturbance in a person's adaptability, either to his environment or to his fellow men, (Figure 76).

PRINT-SCRIPT

In the true sense, "printing" cannot be considered unconnected writing, as it is a copy of the "print," and is not derived from a dissolution of required connections. It is frequently used and even required in certain professions such as engineering, architecture, mechanical drawing, etc.

If print-script is used by adults other than for professional reasons, it takes on a different flavor. Printing is often due to an inability or unwillingness to communicate on a deeper, intimate level, or to face the realities of life. Therefore, printing reflects a facade that hides the true nature of a personality.

For the handwriting analyst, it is not possible to do an in-depth analysis based on printing alone; he should have a sample of "cursive" writing as well.

THE DIFFERENT KINDS OF PRINT-SCRIPTS

There are different kinds of print-scripts; i.e., the block-print which uses all capital letters; print-script employing capital with lower-case letters, and the connected print-script, which uses some connecting strokes.

The Block Print:

The block printers using all capital letters would be the most difficult to analyze, since the writing is confined to the middle zone, which totally eliminates the upper and lower zones, thereby concealing ideas, goals, ambitions, as well as physical and sensual needs. Such people quite often find it difficult to communicate intimately. (Figure 106).

Capital with Small Letters:

The printers who use capital and lower-case letters are better equipped to voice their feelings, since the writing includes all three zones in a limited fashion.

Connected Print-Script:

The connected print-script is often used by students, and later carried into adulthood. On the positive side, it shows the ability for abstract and logical deduction, as well as for creative thinking. Such a printer is making some connections, symbolizing his desire for contact with the YOU, especially if final strokes or words continue to the right. This need for contact may be on a superficial, intellectual level, where his ability to communicate may be excellent. (Figure 108). Large spaces between words and lines indicate detachment and objectivity, but a limited expression of inner feelings.

Mixture of All Types of Printing:

A writing that shows a mixture of the different kinds of printing within one word, or the entire writing sample, is always an indication of uncertainty on the part of the writer as to his or her identity. (Figure 109).

A writing with a mixture of "cursive" and printing has the same meaning. (Figure 110).

REVIEW OF CHARACTERISTICS

Connected writing	logic, conformity.
Connection of several words	laziness, hypomania, the medical term for a state of mania involving abnormal elation and over activity.
Moderately connected with light or medium pressure	tendency for a natural memory.
"i"-dots, "t"-bars connected with the following letter	memory for association, resourcefulness.
"i"-dots, "t"-bars connected backwards and/or forwards	ingenuity, strategic ability, diplomatic inscrutability.
Disconnected capital letters, otherwise connected	pause and reflection between "thinking and doing."
Letters connected to the right instead of the left	simplification; sign of intelligence and expediency.
Unconnected writing	intuition, creativity.
Unconnected writing with inappropriate interruptions	hesitation, uncertainty.
Unconnected, "chopped-up" writing	disturbance in adaptability, mental illness.
Block-printing	difficulty in communicating.
Capital letters with lower-case printing	limited ability to communicate intimately.
Connected print-script	intelligence, abstract thinking, creativity.
Connected print-script with wide spaces	often indicates difficulty in communicating feelings.
Mixture of all types of printing	indecision; uncertainty about own identity.
Mixture of "cursive" writing and printing	indecision; uncertainty about own identity.

Figure 101, Connecting "I-Dots" with Following Letter

This is a sign of intelligence

Figure 102, Connecting Backwards

[signature]

Figure 103, Capital Disconnected

s which Isabel Theory of Types

Figure 104, Unconnected Writing (Painter Goya)

infinito y me ha dicho que se colocaran en Paris en la galeria con singular digni— dad, como merecen, mucha

Figure 105, Unconnected with Inappripriae Interruptions

—Nor must we think that all other feeling. Rather

Figure 106, All Block-Printing

TION — WHAT DOES IT MEAN TO ME?
NOW — BUT REALLY, WHO CARES?!
T THROUGH TWELVE YEARS OF PROBLEM
TIMES, FUN, AND FRIENDSHIPS! BOY,

Figure 107, Print-Script with Capital and Lower-Case Letters

This is a wonderful party.

Having a great time, wish you

Figure 108, Connected Print-Script

Mother opened the garage
door. I would like to
have my handwriting
analyzed. However I would

Figure 109, Mixture of All Types of Printing

SORRY THAT I CANNOT

T YOU AND HAVE A PARTY FOR

KE I ALWAYS DID. I MISS

Figure 110, Mixture of Cursive and Printing

Some Times dear

En joyed our chat

Sent you a Toke

18

The First and Final Letters

THE FIRST LETTER

THE FIRST LETTER OF A WRITTEN WORD SHOWS THE WAY A WRITER FEELS TOWARD new situations and his environment. This is especially revealing if the first letter is the Personal Pronoun "I" (PPI), as it represents our ego and reveals our self-esteem or lack of it. This first letter may be compared to how a person reacts upon entering a room full of people with all the attention focused on him or her.

The different Capital Letters are illustrated on pages 151/152, Figure 110.

THE PERSONAL PRONOUN "I"

The formation and position of the PPI tell much about how we value ourselves. This letter is a measure of our self-confidence. The manner in which it is shaped, its length and fullness relative to the text of the writing, whether emphasized or minimized, simple or entangled, all give valuable clues to the quality of a person's self-worth.

There are literally hundreds of different PPI's, and entire books have been written on that subject, but I will demonstrate and interpret those most frequently encountered. (Pages 153/154, Figure 111).

FINAL LETTERS AND ENDING STROKES

The last letter of a word, and especially its extension, which is called the ending stroke, has a significance all of its own. It can continue to the right, or change direction in a left-ward movement. The last letter may also end abruptly, which is referred to as the "blunt" ending stroke.

Because the writer is generally much more concerned with the first letter and its impression, the last movement is much more indicative of the true nature of a person's feeling and social attitudes.

Another point of interest is the speed, or lack of it. As quick writing is a sign of spontaneity and rapid thought processes, the ending stroke is a genuine reflection of his behavior. Some points which indicate speed of writing are:

- Smooth and rhythmic movements of upstrokes and downstrokes, which form a harmonious pattern, (Figure 56).
- If "i"-dots and "t"-crossings are placed exactly over the respective letter, it is a sign of caution or calculation; this briefly stems the continuity of the movement, whereas in a fast, spontaneous writing, "i"-dots and "t"-bars are generally placed to the right of the letter in a right-handed script. The speed in writing will be further discussed in next chapter.

The various final letters and ending strokes are illustrated on pages 155/156, (Figure 112, a-o).

THE FIRST LETTERS

Figure 110, a-l

a *Boy, I am*

If the capital letter, or PPI, is neither too large nor too small, the person behaves naturally and is not shy; he does not feel he needs to make an impression on others, which is an indication of a secure ego.

b *Todd*

If the first letter is disproportionally high to the rest of the writing, it shows shyness and self-consciousness.

c *Dick*

If the first letter is unusually full and large compared to the rest of the writing, it indicates over-emphasis of self, and is a sign of egotism and a quest for power.

d

Large and very embellished capital letters are an indication of vulgar tastes and ostentation.

e

Initial large loops on capital letters show a desire for responsibility. If the loop is exaggerated, it is a reflection of a domineering personality.

f

A complicated or intricate capital letter is indicative of someone who gets himself into tight or precarious situations, but has the know-how to extricate himself from them.

g *Momma*

Capital letters or other first letters that are made with a "springboard" stroke, often starting from below the base line, are a sign of tension and/or resentment (Figure 94).

h

If a "springboard" upstroke has an initial hook, it intensifies the unconscious aggression or resentment; the hook lends tenacity to these feelings.

i

Printed capital letters are a sign of good taste, which runs toward the simple and uncluttered rather than the ornated style.

j

Capital letters that are bent on the top, leaning farther to the left in a left, and the the right in a right slant, reflect a self-conscious attitude.

k

A lead-in stroke in the form of a gentle wave, which is usually found in "M"s or "N"s is indicative of a good sense of humor.

l

Split capital, or small-case letters, reveal a duplicity in behavior, which may be an indication of mental illness such as schizophrenia, etc.

THE PERSONAL PRONOUN "I"

Figure 111, a-k

a

The adult who retains the copybook "I" is a person who has also kept many traditional values from his early home environment.

b

This is the "cradle" type PPI; it belongs to someone who may not be independent from his parents emotionally and needs much nurturing. Another version of this is the "embryonic" PPI, which has the same interpretation.

c

This is the "tulip" formation. Such a writer is egotistical and secretive about his private life.

d

The "Roman" PPI shows independence and the ability for clear and constructive thinking. This is the PPI often used by engineers, draftsmen, architects.

e

The single stroke PPI shows independence. It belongs topeople who can detach themselves from their personal life if necessary. There may be a lack of feelings.

f

A very tall PPI with a sharp upstroke shows independence and pride; also a sharp penetrating mentality with high goals and ambitions.

g

A similar version of the above but with a leftward arcade at the bottom shows a person who has the tendency to avoid responsibilities and "pass the buck."

h

The PPI resembling the figure "2" reveals that the writer craves possessions in one form or another.

i

This PPI shows a person who has integrated his mother and father image well, and has made his own conscious decisions as to what kind of person and parent he is going to be.

j

The person making this PPI still harbors negative feelings toward his parents. The first stroke symbolized the mother and the second the father image.

k

This is another version of the above.

FINAL LETTERS AND ENDING STROKES

Figure 112, a-o

a

The ending stroke proceeding straight or curved into the upper zone shows interest in religion, mysticism.

b

This is the standard ending stroke, going to the right; it indicates social interest.

c

The ending stroke below the base line shows a fighting spirit and often a hot temper.

d

This is the "blunt" ending letter without extension. If made with pressure, such a person does not tolerate objections well.

e

This sudden change of slant indicates that the person wants to keep others at a distance.

f

Letters that increase in size show a lack of diplomacy. It is often a sign of childishness and immaturity.

g

If the final letter does not return to the base line but hangs in mid-air, it is a sign of insecutiry and/or inhibition.

h

Final letters decreasing in size is a sign of diplomacy and tact.

i

Final letter ending in a "grabbing" hook syas just that; it indicates egotism and "grabbing" all they can.

j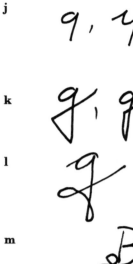

The ending stroke of "g" or "y" in a single stroke without a loop indicates good judgment, but if done weakly, it reveals lack of energy or uncertainty.

k

The "g" loop ending in triangular formation shows aggression and an unyielding spirit.

l

The "g"s or "y"s ending in multiple loop formations shows a peculiarity in sexual habits.

m

The enroled ending stroke shows greed and egotism.

n

The lasso finishing stroke in the upper zone reveals some eccentricity or compulsiveness in habits and ideas.

o

This is the "lyric" finishing stroke. It may be evidenced in the handwriting of poets and musicians.

19

The Importance of
the Small Letters

THE SMALL LETTERS

It would be impossible to show a universal alphabet, because we all have been taught different methods of writing from which we retain certain graphic signs and symbols that become ingrained as permanent fixtures. Generally speaking, the more of these characteristics that are kept and carried into adulthood, the more traditional a person is. A handwriting that adds originality or omits lead-in strokes reflects the individuality of a person.

OMISSION OF LEAD-IN STROKES

This can happen quite early in life, or it may never happen, as it depends largely on the type of personality we possess. Often, people who retain lead-in strokes reveal a greater preoccupation with details than with larger issues, because of the importance that are attached to the former.

The handwriting in Figure 100 belongs to an 18 year old high school graduate who has omitted all of the lead-in strokes, while the writing of Amelia Earhart, the Pacific solo flyer, has retained many upstrokes in small letters, (Figure 113). She certainly had to attach great importance to minute details during her flight. The rest of her writing reveals her spirit of adventure and independence in very high "t"-bars and in the generous word and line spacing.

157

Initial strokes omitted on letters that include the upper zone, such as "t," "l," and "f," which are produced by a single stroke, is an indication of simplification. (See Chapter 14). This is an expression of rapid thought processes, and is generally encountered in the writing of mentally developed individuals.

A writing that shows different letter formations of the same letter reflects the versatility of the writer, if coupled with an even base line, regularity, and other favorable characteristics. If different styles of letters occur in an illegible or "chopped-up" writing with poor rhythm, the interpretation is negative as versatility turns into volatility.

GREEK LETTER FORMATIONS

They are also referred to as "mental formations," because people who chose them possess a facility toward literary expression, (Figure 115 a). These Greek letters are: d, e, g, h, l, k, (Figure 104 - Greek "d"s, "e"s and "g"s). The "g" made like a figure-8 has a special significance. When found in any writing, it reveals the ability to adapt to varied circumstances. Nadya Olyanova states in her book, "Handwriting Tells," that people who make figure 8 "g"s will be equally at home in a tent or a castle, as it is the mark of versatility and flexibility. (Figure 115). Also Figures 101, 104, 108.

HOW WE CROSS OUR "t"s

The "t"-bars are an excellent way of expressing will power, enthusiasm or procrastination. Other horizontal strokes in the writing usually confirm the findings derived from the "t"-crossings.

When different "t"-bars are found in one writing, it is an indication of versatility if coupled with original letter formations, simplification, good word and line spacing, and an even base line, which are all favorable characteristics.

If a variety of "t"-bars are produced where the above features are missing, such as legibility, etc., the interpretation will be negative, as versatility turns into unpredictability. Figure 116 a-o displays the different "t"-bars.

HOW WE DOT OUR "i"s

This is also an excellent indication of our functioning and behavior.

- When the "i"-dots are undotted throughout the writing, it is a sign of poor memory, and it may be seen in the same writing with uncrossed "t"s, although it does not have the identical significance.

- If only some of the "i"s are dotted, it reveals "blind spots," which may be reflected in absent-mindedness, or on a deeper level, the writer may desire to block-out certain experiences from his mind. The latter would be confirmed when lower zone loops do not return to the base line, which gives a clue that the writer is suppressing something. Figure 117 a-g shows the different kinds of "i"-dots.

THE SPEED OF WRITING

I have already touched on the factor of speed or the lack of it in previous chapters. Speed in writing is an expression of uninterrupted thought processes, which proceed smoothly and evenly from one word to another. (See Figures 56, 61, 65, 75, 100).

When a person is unable to concentrate fully on what he is thinking and writing at that moment, and other matters keep interfering, it slows down the writing process.

- Slow and laborious writing may be the result of over-control of the impulses, which is a sign of repression. Such a person uses up most of his precious energies to keep them in check. This results in loss of spontaneity, seen in Figure 68. Corroborating factors of an excess in control include an even base line and squeezed narrowness in the writing; the former is a favorable feature because it keeps the individual on an "even keel" and well-functioning - at least on the surface.

- Figure 105 is another slow writing sample, but contrary to the previous one, this writing is marked with interruptions, mendings and retracings, all slowing down the rhythm and flow of writing. In addition, the "smeary and pasty" ductus, which will be further discussed in the next chapter on "Pressure," describes an entirely different individual from the one in Figure 68.

The above characteristics are all negative indicators, and in slow writing they give evidence of calculated dishonesty. The encircled letter formations and the dish-shaped "t"-crossings, (Figure 116 l), all point to sexual overindulgence and possessiveness, which is revealed in the tightly knotted loops. This writer would like to give an impression of sophistication, while he actually exemplifies vulgarity.

Figure 113, Rataining Some Lead-In Strokes. (Amelia Earhart)

STANDARD AND ORIGINAL LETTER FORMATIONS

Figure 114, a-s

a   Letters open at the top show generosity if found in a rhythmic writing.

b   Letters that open at the bottom are rare, but they are a sign of insincerity and dishonesty.

c   Tightly closed "a"s or "o"s indicate caution, also a measure of secretiveness, which can be a positive feature, because such people can be trusted with a secret.

d   An open lip of the "b" suggest a trusting attitude with a tendency to be gullible.

e   Closed "b"s in standard or simplified formations show business sense and good judgment.

f   These "t" formations are stubborn types; they show an open space between the up and downstrokes which often finishes below the base line. This intensifies the stubbornness.

g   Tall, retraced "d" stems show pride and dignity, but it can also reveal a "better-than-thou" attitude.

h   These "f" formations show simplification; they indicate artistic leanings and a sense for the aesthetic.

i 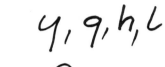

The absence of loops in these letters express good judgment and concentration.

j 

Wide upper loops in these letters shows sensitivity and perception, and often indicates musical ability.

k k, k

The absence of loops is a form of simplification, reflecting abstract thinking and cultural leanings. If the "k" is made with a large buckle, the writer likes to be in charge of things, which can be interpreted either positively or negatively, depending on other confirming characteristics.

m m, n

Rounded tops of these letters show a lack of mental acuity, which may also express immaturity. If made by children, arcaded "m"s are normal.

n m, n

Garland connection with sharp upper points on "n"s or "m"s combine sociability with mental sharpness.

p P, P

This letter with a long and full loop is often called the "physical p." It may also be made without a loop, but with a long extension and pressure.

q q

This is the simplified version of the letter, and is a sign of altruism and expediency.

q

The letter first attempting to turn right and then changing direction to the left tells of the writer's impulse to give which is overruled by caution or a change of heart.

r

These are broad "r"s, which always point to a strong visual sense. Such a person usually knows how to put into practice what he sees; it is often found among artists, architects and dress designers.

These are quick "r"s, which show fast thinking.

s

These formations are often seen in the same writing as the closed "a"s and "o"s, bearing the same significance.

GREEK LETTER FORMATIONS

Figure 115, a & b

a

These are often referred to as "mental formations." Where encountered, they point to a facility toward lieterary expression.

b

The "g" made like a figure-8 has a special significance. When found in any hand, it shows a high degree of adaptability with regard to people and circumstances. It is also a sign of versatility and flexibility.

THE DIFFERENT "t" BARS

Figure 116, a-o

a

This is the precise "t"-bar placed directly above the letter. It indicates good attention to detail and dependability.

b

The "t"-bar to the left of the stem shows procrastination and indecision. This person starts a project, but does not carry out his intentions.

c

The "t"-bar which is tied or crossed low on the stem of the letter shows someone who does not openly assert himself; such a person is always giving in to other people's demands.

d

These "t"-bars indicate ambition, enthusiasm and nervous energy, and may also reflect hastiness.

e

Hooks on "t"-bars, either at the beginning or the end, or on both, reveals persistence and determination. It also shows varius degrees of possessiveness.

f

Downward slanting "t"-bars are indicative of a critical disposition which may be expressed in fault-finding or a quarrelsome disposition. It also reflects sarcasm if the starting point of the "t"-bar is heavier than at the end.

g

Where the ending point of the bar is heavier than at the beginning, resembling a club, it is an indication of a brutal temper. If the writing shows heavy pressure or smeariness, such a person can be physically aggressive.

h

Rising "t"-bars show ambition, imagination and enthusiasm. It will depend on other factors, such as the forms of connections, pressure, etc., how these "t"-crossings are interpreted.

i

Bowed "t"-bars show a measure of self-discipline, especially if placed firmly and directly over the stem. This may be found in the writing of athletes, pilots, etc.

j

Crossings above the stem is a sign of adventure; it may also indicate very high goals, some of which might be unattainable. The rest of the writing will tell whether these "t"-bars belong to the "dreamer" or the adventurer.

k

These are ineffectual "t"-bars, either crossed or uncrossed. If the bar is lighter than the pressure in the rest of the text, it shows weakness of will and indecision.

l

These types of "t"-bars show willfulness and self-indulgence, also in the sexual area.

m

Looped or tied "t"-bars, as in all letter formations, are a sign of persistence, and may also show peculiarities in personal habits.

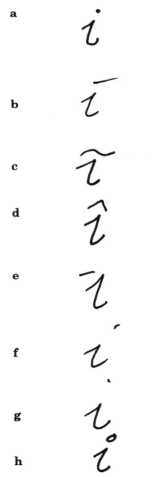

n

These are called the "star-shaped-bars." They show extreme sensitivity toward one-self. This is a combination of the procrastination "t"-bar and the aggressive formation. If the bar does not cross the stem but flies above it, it may indicate a lack of realism.

o

The "t-bar" which turns to the left and stays there is a form of self-protection and introversion, even if found with opposite (extroverted characteristics. (Figure 85).

THE DIFFERENT "i" DOTS

Figure 117, a-h

a

Firmly dotted exactly above the letter shows careful attention to detail, and a good memory for facts and figures. It may be found in the writing with "t"-bars crossed precisely in the middle of the stem.

b

When made with heavy pressure, the writer is aggressive and is likely to have a hot temper.

c

Wavy lines as "i"-dots are called "laughing mouths," and are a sign of good humor.

d

Tent-shaped dots show a critical mind, which often goes together with angular writing.

e

The "i"-dot to the left of the letter shows caution, indecision and procrastination, similar to "t"-bars that crossed to the left of the stem.

f

The "i"-dot to the right of the stem is a sign of speed, and shows enthusiasm and nervous energy.

g

The highly placed "i"-dot is a sign of imagination.

h

The circle "i"-dots are a bid for attention.

20

The Pressure in Writing

WHAT TYPE OF PEN DO YOU USE?

THE PRESSURE IN HANDWRITING DEPENDS ON THE PHYSICAL AND PSYCHOLOGICAL strength that the writer exerts on the writing surface. It also depends on what type of pen is being used.

A ballpoint or fountain pen creates a deeper indentation or furrow than the pens with a broader nib. Markers of various degrees of thicknesses give a broader appearance. Genuine pressure can be estimated correctly by turning the page and feeling the indentations. In this way, one can also observe uneven or erratic pressure in writing.

People who prefer the sharp ballpoint pen actually like to feel resistance between the pen and the paper. Angular writers most likely choose this type of pen over the broad nibs, even for the reason that angles are easier to manage with a sharp pen or tool. Generally speaking, people who deal with facts and figures in their professions, such as engineering, accounting, mathematics and physics, unconsciously select a pen that produces a sharper ductus. (Figure 56 - Albert Einstein). This also applies to people who see things more in terms of "black-and-white" or "right-or-wrong." (Figure 118). Individuals who deal with human nature, such as psychologists, social workers, sales related professions, artists, etc., are apt to see "shades-of-gray." (Figure 119 - French Impressionist painter Claude Monet).

Some people even choose different pens for different occasions. I write with a ballpoint pen when making notes or writing drafts, and automatically switch to a broader nibbed pen when writing a personal letter, in which case my writing not only is larger and wider, it also uses a more generous amount of space.

THE PRESSURE IN WRITING

As mentioned above, the pressure exerted on the writing surface is not merely a manifestation of the physical, but of psychological or mental energies, and therefore, is a reflection of the will as well as of creative power. Pressure adds a third dimension to the handwriting.

The most favorable pressure is a "shaded" movement of upstrokes and downstrokes; with the former lighter than the latter. This creates a rhythmic pattern of lighter and darker writing, which symbolizes "tension and release."

If such writing is not merely like the monotonous product of a well-oiled machine, but is made by the introduction of original letter formations, and a variety of connections such as garlands, angles, arcades and thread, we refer to it as a "high form level" writing.

The sample in Figure 100 is the handwriting of a young man of 18 who shows excellent potential for such a high form level. The writing in Figure 75 is that of a mature doctor of medicine, professor, author and specialist, who exemplifies this high form level, evidenced by the mixture of connections, simplification and "Greek mental formations," discussed in the previous chapter.

Heavy Pressure:

This shows a high intensity of energy produced by willpower or physical force. Pressure is like a release valve. As mentioned above, this can only be evaluated correctly from the backside of the page and from an original writing sample, not from a copy.

- If heavy pressure is released, coupled with some measure of self-control, seen in a straight base line, moderately regular writing and slant, it signifies that the person is not controlled by his emotions, but rather that he has the control over them, in which case heavy pressure is an indication of powerful energy. (Figure 113 - Amelia Earhart).

- If these favorable characteristics are lacking in a heavy-pressure writing, the interpretation must be negative. Such a person may be dominated by unchecked psychological emotions such as fears, anger, resentment, etc., which work destructively on a personality, or it may be a sign of mental illness. (Figure 120).

- Heavy pressure in angular writing, such as that in Figure 95, is an indication of physical aggression and brutality. It is the signature of the notorious German sadist Julius Streicher.

Medium Pressure:

Again, both the front and backside of the writing should be examined to determine the pressure.

- A writing with medium pressure and good rhythm, dotted "i"s and crossed "t"s is a sign of a good memory. For some reason, heavy pressure is not as conducive to a natural memory as medium to light pressure in a favorable writing.

- Medium pressure in writing also reveals reasonably fast thinking processes and good concentration, provided that the writing has the above mentioned prerequisites.

- Individuals who apply medium pressure are not as intense as those who write with heavy pressure. That is not to say that they don't feel things keenly, but not with the same intensity, which allows them to be more objective and detached. Medical doctors or nurses, for instance, would benefit from having a medium pressure in their writing.

Light Pressure:

The positive characteristics of light pressure is the ability to perceive new things rapidly and to assess situations quickly. The necessary prerequisites are a straight base line, moderate regularity in letter formations and slant, and adequate spacing between words and lines discussed in the next chapter. These features will lend realism and stability to the light pressured writing. In some way, the light pressure is a defense mechanism, because people who have been hurt emotionally in the past, usually originating in childhood experiences, feel the need to keep things at a distance or to let them "roll off their backs" without penetrating too deeply into their psyche. If light pressure is coupled with a left slant, it would confirm this diagnosis. (Figure 121).

Light pressure in a very irregular writing that shows neglect in the middle and lower zones indicates diminished energy, which is often accompanied by descending letter formations. (Figure 122).

Light pressure coupled with much irregularity and signs of haste may be an indication of hysteria or other forms of neurotic conditions. (Figure 97).

REGULARITY VERSUS IRREGULARITY

Regularity:

I have mentioned these two characteristics in previous chapters. They are complex, and not easy to define.

Just as "regularity" is a sign of control and is a favorable feature in moderation, in excess it shows a lack of spontaneity that keeps the writer from embarking on new ventures and challenges, or experiencing maximum enjoyment of life. A writing has to strike a balance between regularity and irregularity.

- Regularity in a garland writing or mixed connections reflect a person who is well adapted, and is not afraid to tackle new things. He or she is comfortable in social situations. (Figures 65 and 89).

- A slow, squeezed and narrow writing with extreme regularity and an even base line shows over-control and/or inhibition. With that much self-discipline applied, the writing gives a stiff and monotonous appearance. Such an individual spends too much of his vital energy toward self-control, which does not allow full enjoyment of life. (Figure 68).

Irregularity:

This is the opposite of regularity and indicates a lack of self-control in one area or another. The sample in Figure 93 is the writing of a 18 year old high school graduate; it shows irregularity pertaining to size, slant, base line and letter formations, all of which point to the fact that this young lady is not focused on anything at this time. It not only indicates uncertainty in direction and her own identity, but also a lack of maturity. Comparing this writing with those of other high school graduates in Figures 61, 62, 65, 84, 89, 92, 100, who are exceptionally mature for their age, this girl's writing suggests conflicts that may be a part of the growing-up process.

Figure 118, Sharp Writing

Figure 119, Pastose Writing (Impressionist Painter Claude Monet)

Figure 120, Heavy Pressure, Lack of Control

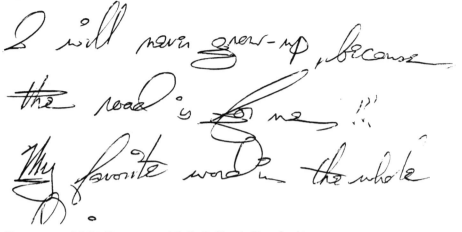

Figure 121, Light Pressure with Left Slant, Regularity

Figure 122, Light Pressure, Irregularity, Neglect

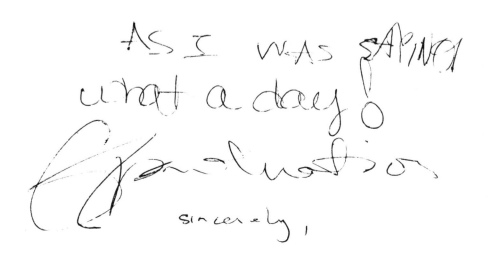

21

The Margins

THE MARGINS

THE STRUCTURE OF THE HANDWRITING DEPENDS NOT ONLY ON LETTER FORMA-
TIONS and the spacing between words and lines, but also on the ar-
rangement and format of the given writing space. This "unused" space
consists of four margins: top, bottom, left and right. The left and right
margins are the most significant.

The Top and Bottom Margins:

- Leaving an ample upper margin reveals respect for the ad-
dressee, while a small or non-existent one conveys the opposite.
The latter may also indicate a lack of thought and planning,
which are often a reflection of youthful inconsideration and immaturity.

- A non-existent lower margin is scarcely noticed. Quite often,
the writer concentrating on his communication hates to interrupt
his train of thought by either turning the page or starting a new
one, which shows that the intensity of communicating his mes-
sage overrides his sense of the aesthetic. This person is apt to
make his own rules rather than to follow prescribed ones.

- If an ample bottom margin is present, the writer has a developed sense of the aesthetic which is the dominant factor. It also
expresses a generous attitude or largesse where material things
are concerned.

The Left Margin:

The left margin symbolizes the "past," the "mother image" and the "self," and therefore is of special significance.

- A sufficient left margin is an expression of cultural, aesthetic and material standards. It also reveals the necessary emotional detachment from parents as we become adults. This does not mean "estrangement" from family; rather, it shows maturity and independence to make our own choices in life. In the true sense, it symbolizes the "cutting of the umbilical cord." Some people never manage to do this, and some parents never encourage it. (Figure 123 a).

- If the left margin is smaller than the right, it shows someone more concerned about the past and where he is coming from than where he is going, which reveals a lack of orientation toward the future. (Figure 123 b).

- The lack of left or right margin expresses thriftiness if found in a small or narrow writing. Such a person does not believe in wasting space, which is his dominant "modus operandi." (Figure 123 c).

- It seems a strange paradox that in a large ego-expressing handwriting, the lack of margins is the sign of a "spendthrift" who wants to have it all.

- The convex left margin is indicative of a person who exhibits a generosity which is not consistent. Presently, he resumes his natural thriftiness. (Figure 123 d).

- The concave margin suggests that the writer resolves to economize, but can't keep it up. After some time, his self-control and discipline to curtail spending takes over again. (Figure 123 e).

- The usage of space, where the left margin keeps getting larger and larger, shows an initial reserve and resolve at economy which is not kept up. (Figure 123 f).

- The zig-zag margin shows a person's struggles between demands and attempts at self-control in spending. The writer is also inconsistent in his attitudes and behavior. (Figure 123 g).

- A completely missing left margin with a wide right one shows someone who is extremely introverted and is only comfortable with family and close friends. This person has "not left home yet," regardless of his chronological age.

This formation of the margins may be an indication of "street fear" which is called "agoraphobia." (Figure 123 h).

The Right Margin:

This margin symbolizes the future, and in a sense represents the "father image." It also reflects a person's attitudes toward the "you" and with the world-at-large, which is further expressed in the final letters and ending strokes. Someone could be future-oriented without being too interested in the welfare of others; he may be adventurous and have many goals and interests which do not necessarily involve personal or intimate contact with others.

- A non-existent right margin indicates that a person is extremely people and/or world-oriented; if the former is the case, it will be indicated by ending strokes that continue to the right in a predominantly right-slanted writing. If these features are absent in the writing, such an individual is more cause-oriented. (Figure 124 - a non-existent right margin).

- A person who uses only the middle of the available space reveals feelings of isolation, which is a form of self-protection. This is quite often the result of a conscious or unconscious vulnerability. (Figure 124 b).

THE ADDRESS ON THE ENVELOPE

It is a point of interest to compare the text of the letter with the address on the envelope. The writing in the text may be congruent (identical) to the one on the envelope, or it may vary greatly in size, slant and even in style.

- If the address on the envelope is written with more care than the text, it indicates that the sender pays greater attention to his outer appearance than to his private self, because the address reflects the outer image a person likes to convey, while the text is a reflection of his inner disposition. However, a clearly written and legible address is always an indication of the writer's consideration for authority; he wants to make sure that his letter is being delivered.

- Embellishments and increased right slant on the envelope speaks for generous gestures and an outgoing personality which, unless they are supported in the text of the letter, are of a superficial nature.

- If the address shows tendencies to the left, while the text of the letter is right-slanted, it reflects an initial reserve or inhibition which disappears when the person "warms up."

- If both the address and the text are written identically in size, slant and style, one can assume that the person behaves naturally, and does not feel the need to put up a false front or facade.

THE DISTRIBUTION OF THE SPACE

The spacial distribution - where the address is placed on the envelope - is significant, but this is also subject to the customs and regulations of each country. Assuming that we are looking at a private letter, the envelope is divided into four equal quadrants. (Figure 125).

- The upper right corner is reserved for the stamps. If the writer is using this for the address, it shows an inconsiderate attitude and reflects youthful insouciance. Such a usage of space can indicate rebelliousness and conflicts with rules and authority, which may disappear with growing maturity.

- When the address is written in steps from the upper left to the lower right, it is an expression of caution or reserve. Such a writer is often hesitant or not at ease with people other than the ones he knows. This type of formation on the address seems standard procedure among the British, which may reflect a "national characteristic" of reserve.

- An address that is written in steps from the right to the left is rare, but I have such a friend who consistently forms her address in this fashion. Although she seems outgoing and eager for contact with people on a social level, there must be an element in her past that has a strong hold on her. (Figure 126).

- A predominant usage of the upper left quadrant on the envelope shows inhibition in some area of this person's life. He or she wants to avoid the progress to the right, which symbolizes the future. Such an attitude most probably is rooted in a childhood, where the child was afraid to face certain situations or problems.

Figure 123, a-h

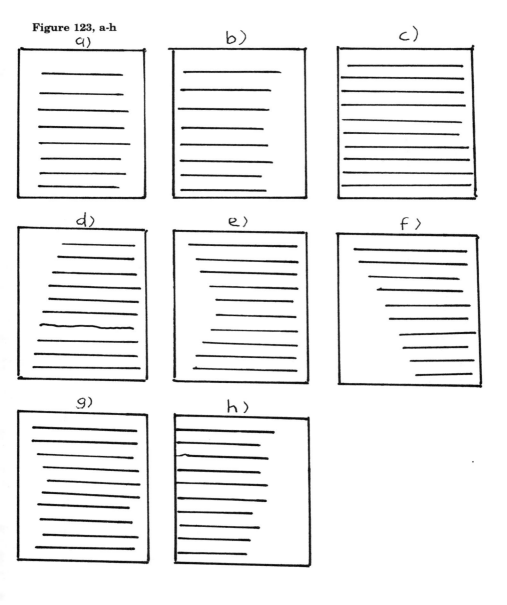

Figure 124, a-b

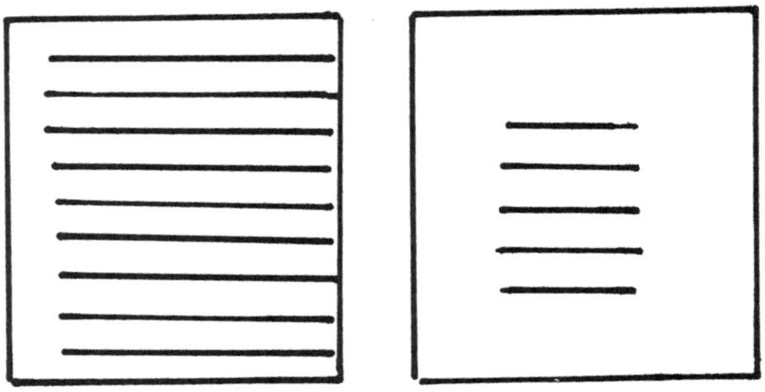

Figure 125, The Four Quadrants

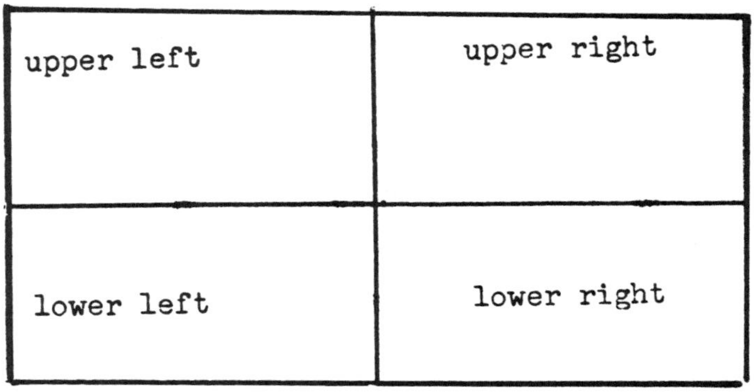

upper left	upper right
lower left	lower right

Figure 126, Address Written in Steps from Right to Left

22

The Signature

GRAPHOLOGICALLY SPEAKING, THE SIGNATURE CONSISTS OF FIRST NAME, MIDDLE initial, and the family name. Sometimes the signature finishes with an optional "underscore" that has a special significance. Since there are literally thousands of different formations, some indicate peculiarities. (Figure 130 - Joan Crawford, Figure 134 - Andy Warhol).

BUSINESS SIGNATURES

One should distinguish between official and personal signatures. Businessmen and officials who have to affix their signatures to hundreds of letters and documents quite often select a "trademark-type" of signature; this is especially prevalent among diplomatic circles. However, even those trademark configurations are unique. In many ways, quite unknown to the writer, they reveal a great deal about him, which may be the opposite of his intentions. (Figures 127 and 128).

GENERAL CHARACTERISTICS

- Signatures that are congruent with the text belong to people who have the courage to stand by their word, whether in business or in private life.

- An increased size of the first name, or a very large capital letter, shows egotism and is a reflection of someone who is "power-hungry." Figure 129 shows part of a letter by Richard Nixon that exemplifies this characteristic. Notice his huge capital "D." Another excellent example is Joan Crawford's signature, which not only reveals hunger for power but expresses deceit, seen in hidden letters and the "tulip" formation in the oversized "J." She totally over-emphasized her own importance, confirmed in her underscored signature. (Figure 130).

- If the signature is smaller than the text, the writer is more modest and unpretentious than he appears.

- Illegible signatures may be a "trademark," as described above, or they may indicate an avoidance of responsibilities, (Figure 127). This includes people whose signatures are totally different in style from the text, which is a form of disguise, or it may point to someone who leads a double life.

- A person who makes a distinction between his official and private signature is likely to have different standards of ethics.

- Strokes in the signature that are extended to the left into the upper zone express cultural remembrances. They may appear in signatures of poets as well as in those who have an interest in history and/or antiques, etc. Through experience, I have found this to be accurate, especially if found in writings that otherwise are more oriented toward the future than the past.

- Strokes that are extended to the left in the lower zone relates to the past with regard to sexual or material matters. (Figure 130).

- Ascending signatures are a sign of enthusiasm or ambition. There is little doubt that the writing in Figure 127 indicates ambition, rather than enthusiasm, confirmed by the angularity and tension that are evident in the signature.

- Descending strokes in signatures, or in any other part, are a sign of fatigue, illness or discouragement. Figure 131 shows the signature of Adolph Hitler, which reveals discouragement or fatigue, as well as a degree of sadism in the smeary ductus. Figure 132 is the signature of a musically talented person who admitted to being easily depressed.

- People who set periods after their name, or to the left of it, have acquired a measure of caution and suspicion. They also like to have the last word. Note the powerful, aggressive and colorful signature of Lyndon Johnson.

- Names that are completely encircled by a final stroke express a desire for privacy, or the hiding of plans. Such people do not like others to look into their business or private life, which they often keep jealously guarded. Figure 134 is the signature of painter Andy Warhol.

- Club-like final strokes in signatures are the same as elsewhere; they indicate a tendency toward physical force, while sharp final strokes reflect intellectual sharpness. Figure 135 depicts one of the signatures of John (Jack) Kennedy with such sharp final strokes in the upper zone.

- The lassoes as final strokes in the upper zone are an indication of fetishes or eccentricities in personal habits, while lassoes in the lower zone express calculated cleverness that captures those around the individual, through either charm or cunning. (Figure 136 - Actress Jane Seymour and Figure 148, Marilyn Monroe).

- Signatures that are made with a final stroke under the name, whether attached or unconnected, are referred to as "underscored." Such strokes always signify the writer's intention to emphasize his own importance. The underscored signature in Figure 130 reveals aggression by the sharpness of the left-ward movement.

Figure 127, Business Signature

Very truly yours,

Figure 128, Business or Personal

Figure 129, Very Large Capital Letter in First Name (Richard Nixon)

Figure 130, Egotism/Deceit

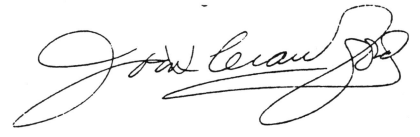

Figure 131, Descending Signature; Depression/Sadism (Adolf Hitler)

Figure 132, Descending Signature

Figure 133, Periods in Signature of Former President Lyndon B. Johnson

| **Figure 134, Encircled Signature** | **Figure 135, Sharp Final Downstroke** |
| (Andy Warhol) | (John F. Kennedy) |

Figure 136, Lasso Formation in Lower Loops (Jane Seymour)

Cordially,

Jane Seymour

23

Spacing and Rhythm

SPACING BETWEEN WORDS

A VERY IMPORTANT FACTOR OF THE INDIVIDUAL RHYTHM IN HANDWRITING IS THE spacing of words and lines. Not only the writing is significant, but the "unused" space or distances between words and lines, as well as the four margins, as described in Chapter 9. Normal spacing between words consists of the width of one letter, taking into consideration the particular fullness or narrowness of the writing, which means that the space between words in a narrow writing should be smaller than that in a wide or full writing. Any spacing that deviates from this guide line is referred to as either "too wide" or "insufficient". The larger the distances between the words, the more the "creative pause" reflects a "gap," which is interpreted as a sign of caution or isolation.

- Adequate spacing between words shows good organizational skills. Such a person expresses logical thought processes that allow the individual to function satisfactorily in day-to-day living. (Figure 138).
- When the distance between the words are too wide, they are referred to as "gaps" or "rivers," and reflect shyness, caution or isolation. The rest of the writing will confirm which is applicable, evidenced in final letters, ending strokes and margins. (Figure 139 a and 139 b - Amelia Earhart).

- Small writing with large distances between words show the critical observer. (Figure 140).

- Large writing with large intervals between words is a manifestation of self-esteem. Such a person considers himself of primary importance. (Figure 141).

- Insufficient word spacing is often found in very spontaneous writing. People who are naturally judicious provide for adequate spacing that does not impair the speed or the continuity of its movement. Inadequate spacing is often an indication of the impulse dominating the intellect. These individuals have a tendency to infringe on other people's privacy, and they hate to be alone. (Figure 142).

- Irregular spacing expresses fluctuating and unpredictable or inconsistent behavior. (Figure 143).

THE LINE SPACING

In examples of sufficient line spacing, upper and lower strokes and loops do not entangle or interfere with the lines from above or below. It is also important to note that an average spacing between words does not automatically include the same for the lines as demonstrated in Figure 137. While the word spacing reflects the daily functioning of an individual, the line spacing shows planning and objectivity on a larger scale.

-    Clear spacing of the lines is an indication of objective thinking and reasoning, which also includes planning of larger issues. Good word and line spacing, therefore, is a sign of common sense and intelligence that reflects good organizational skills in all areas of functioning. (Figure 144).

- Where the line spacing would be adequate except for abnormally long lower zonal loops, it shows a reduced faculty for objectivity, as demonstrated in Figure 145.

- If the lines are entangled from above and below in a network of crossing loops and strokes, it is obvious that objective and clear reasoning is almost impossible. Such a person will get priorities mixed up where emotions, sensual and material needs are concerned. (Figure 146).

- A line spacing that is too wide does not indicate increased objectivity, rather it expresses a lack of realism in some area. (Figure 140).

RHYTHM IN HANDWRITING

Natural rhythm is the undisturbed flow of upstrokes and downstrokes and of words and lines. Harmonious and even distribution expresses only that, biologically, the writing impulse is not impaired or disturbed. Such a rhythmic writing without the expression of individuality or vitality appears as a monotonous fluid movement of graphic symbols, which may be produced by either a "mindless robot" or by someone who functions with maximum precision like a well-oiled machine. The writing in Figure 147 was not made by a mindless robot, but rather by a person who is focusing on a specific task or goal with intense concentration and efficiency, seen in the heavy pressure and right slanted script. Such a person has shut out much of his vitality and self-expression in order to function with utmost expediency in one area.

We speak of the "individual" rhythm as that by which a writing is as recognizable as the face of a person. Even during illness or changes in life, the individual rhythm may be retained.

- Figure 148 shows the handwriting of Marilyn Monroe which exhibits self-expression and vitality. The presence of such an individual rhythm does not necessarily include a balanced personality. In her writing, the upper, and especially the lower zone, are out of proportion to the middle zone. This overemphasis in the lower sphere expresses her continuous need for attention and adoration from those around her, which was surely the result of a childhood without a father figure, for which she craved her entire life, confirmed in her long lower-zone loops turning back to the left. The middle zone is comparatively "meager," which shows an exacting quality, also expressed in the many hooks throughout the writing that reveal possessiveness.

Disturbed Rhythm:

Strange as it may seem, the severely irregular writing in Figure 149 has a very strong "individual" rhythm, revealing vitality seen in originality of expression and good humor strokes in the "M" and "N." What is absent in this writing is "normal" rhythm. The writing reflects considerable irregularities in size, slant, letter formations and especially in the uneven base line. This is an indication that this man of over sixty is disorganized, but that he still functions reasonably well in the social area, which is evidenced in the large size of the writing, good word spacing and ending strokes to the right. This sample exemplifies the point that I am trying to make; i.e., that the individuality of the rhythm can be retained regardless of diminished mental capacities or age.

HARMONY AND BALANCE

Since the handwriting is an expression of our physical, mental and spiritual impulses, it is a reflection of our total personality. Disharmony or disruption in any of these areas produces graphic signs of imbalance or ambivalence that may be of temporary duration. We all know that our writing can fluctuate from day to day, depending on our moods and state of mind. While the contents of a written communication is affected largely by the conscious will of the individual, the writing's forms and spacial distribution are an unconscious and automatic reflection of our personality and character. Its values can only be properly evaluated by a complete, step-by-step analysis, balancing and weighing each finding against another.

It is my hope that my introduction into graphology has engendered sufficient interest for you, the reader, to embark on further studies of that subject.

P.S. I would like to mention that the handwriting samples of Albert Einstein, Marilyn Monroe, Amelia Earhart, and the signatures of Nelsen Rockefeller and John F. Kennedy were copied from the book "Handwriting Tells," by Nadya Olyanova. This book is currently reprinted by the Whilshire Book Company, 12015 Sherman Road, North Hollywood, CA 91605.

Figure 137, Sufficient Word Spacing; Insufficient Line Spacing

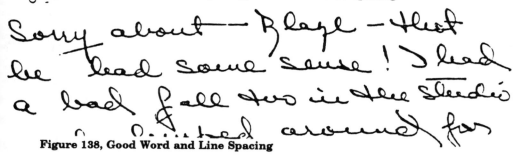

Sorry about — Blagh — that
be lead some sense! I had
a bad fall too in the studio
Puttered around for

Figure 138, Good Word and Line Spacing

NIGHT SKY, CARRYING THE BRIDAL BOUQUET!
GOLDSCHMIOT GET REALLY EXCITED OVER THAT!
DON'T KNOW QUITE WHEN WE WILL GET BACK TO
CALIFORNIA, THOUGH I HOPE IT IS SOON. MEANWH
—AND, AS ALWAYS — OUR KINDEST REGARDS.

Figure 139 a, Word Spacing Too Wide; "Gaps"

I find graduation very
exciting and I can't
wait to go to college.

Figure 139 b, Word Spacing Too Wide (Amelia Earhart)

The take-off is gene
del as the most ?
of the flight. I can

Figure 140, Small Writing with Large Word Spacing

I am very psyched to have graduated. I look forward to college and meeting new people, b

Figure 141, Large Writing with Large Word Spacing

Will My Writing Great
I's And My's Do The
Service You Want. Rendered

Figure 142, Insufficient Word Spacing

we made it. Your I will
just sit back and relax
will party and fun too
I am also looking forwr

Figure 143, Irregular Word Spacing

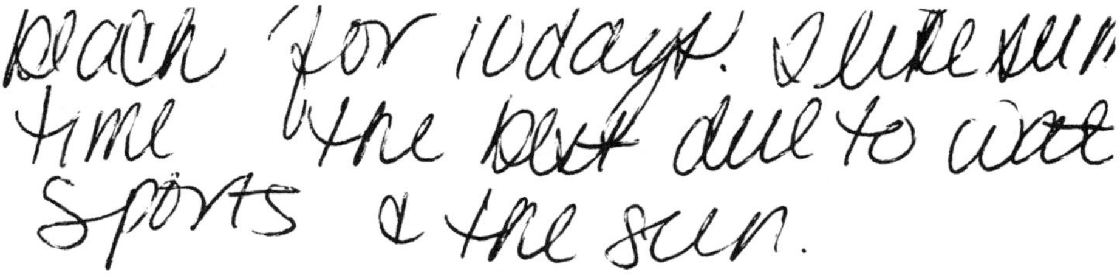

beach for 10 days. I like sun time 4 the best due to watt sports & the sun.

Figure 144, Clear Word and Line Spacing

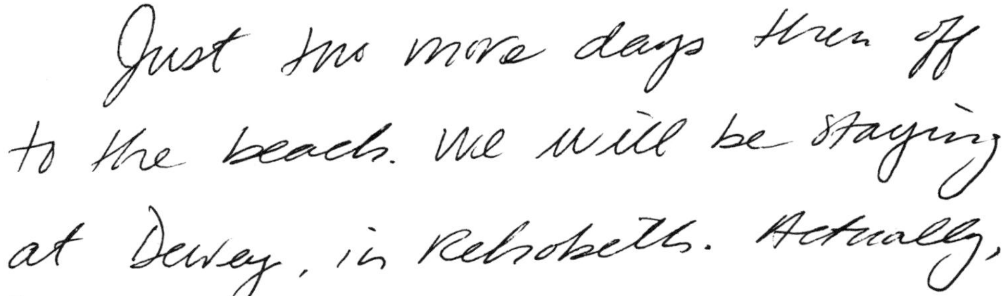

Just two more days then off to the beach. We will be staying at Dewey, in Rehobeth. Actually,

Figure 145, Good Word Spacing. Lower Zone Loops Interference

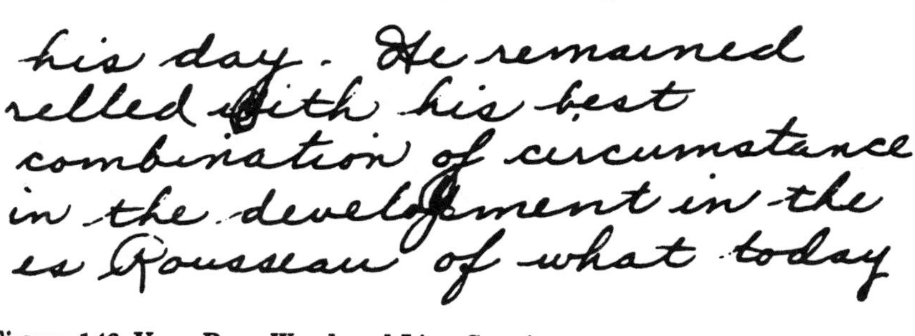

his day. He remained relled with his best combination of circumstance in the development in the es Rousseau of what today

Figure 146, Very Poor Word and Line Spacing

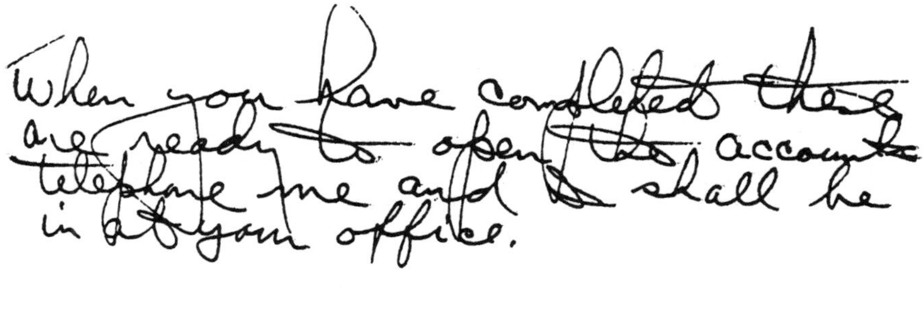

When you have completed these are ready to open the account telephone me and I shall be in at your office.

Figure 147, Monotonous Rhythmic Writing

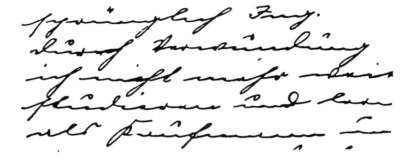

Figure 148, Individual Rhythm (Marilyn Monroe)

Writing sample from the book "Handwriting Tells" by Nadya Olyanova

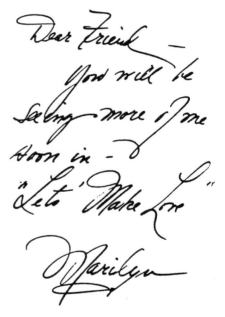

Figure 149, Irregular Writing, Strong Individual Rhythm

PART FOUR

Interpreting the Hand & Writing Together

☆

The correlation and interrelation of the hands
and handwriting.

Personality profiles and career aptitudes.

24

Zonal Division

THE PALMAR SURFACE, FINGERS AND THUMB, AS WELL AS THE HANDWRITING, CAN be divided into three zones, i.e., the mental/spiritual, emotional/social, and the physical/instinctual spheres. In the hand, it is important to note the proportions of the zones and finger sections. Any deviation from the "normal," such as exaggeration of one area by short-changing the others, shows that one feature may be the dominating, driving force of the personality and its "modus operandi." (PART I, Chapter 3, 4, and PART II, Chapter 7).

The zonal division is equally significant in the handwriting. (PART III, Chapter 13). Good balance of the three zones generally points to harmony that is tantamount to a balanced and well-adjusted personality. If good rhythm, originality, and signs of intelligence are added to good zonal balance, it is an expression of the highest form of human or intellectual potential.

Discrepancies or contradictory indicators can manifest themselves in any of the three zones and point to a person's ambivalence or idiosyncrasies without necessarily decreasing his ability to function.

In the case of printing, especially if "block-printing" is used, the upper and lower zones are obliterated. By emphasizing the middle zone, the writer accentuates his daily functioning and professional life, thus consciously or subconsciously hiding his private domain or feelings behind a facade.

THE MENTAL/PERCEPTUAL ZONE
In the Hand: (Figure 150)

The various functions of the fingers, thumb and the palm were discussed in detail in PART I, Chapters 3 and 4, and PART II, Chapter 7, respectively. Mental/spiritual perception is gleaned not only from the top sections of fingers and the thumb, but also from the upper section of the palm.

- The Jupiter finger represents leadership, world-directedness and a desire for responsibility. If the finger itself is long compared to the Saturn and Apollo fingers, and its tip section is also long, these qualities are further enhanced. If Jupiter is short, with a shorter than average top phalange, it would have the opposite interpretation. Such a person would shy away from being in charge of other people's affairs, and the chances exist that he would have little interest in the world-at-large.

- The Saturn finger represents religious fervor, interest in law and order, and love of home and stability. If this finger is well-proportioned and in good balance with Jupiter and Apollo, a person's seriousness and lightheartedness are balanced equally. But if this finger, especially the top phalange, is of exceptional length, serious qualities are enhanced. Such an individual's nature borders on the melancholic/depressive, as he looks upon the negative and darker side of things. This personality type is sometimes referred to as "Saturnian."

A comparatively short finger of Saturn with a short top phalange would have the opposite interpretation; i.e., a lack of seriousness and disregard for law and authority.

- The Apollo finger reflects not only our creative forces, but our social attitudes. A well-proportioned finger, compared to Saturn and Jupiter, shows inborn social instincts. If the finger and its top section are shorter than average, such a person is either unaware of the creative forces within himself or he is not allowing them to surface. An exceptionally long Apollo finger with a long top phalange is a form of exaggeration that, being extreme, is a negative feature, as it indicates a tendency toward gambling and foolhardiness.

- The Mercury finger is "the messenger" or communicator, and relates to the communication of the spoken or written word, which includes the ability to express it in music. A long finger and top phalange enhance these qualities, and therefore is an asset to have for sales people, teachers, public speakers, etc. A long fingertip also indicates persuasiveness, which further enhances the success in these and other professions. A low-set or twisted Mercury decreases its favorable qualities, as a low-set finger reveals lack of self-confidence, while the twisted finger is a sign of a "twisted mentality" unless the malformation was caused by injury.

Mercury is also the messenger that speaks of intimate relationships. A twisted finger often reflects unfavorable relationships with parents, which can lead to conflicts with later ones.

- The Thumb, as discussed in PART I, Chapter 4, is of the utmost importance. A long and strong one attests to perseverance and staying power. Its top section represents the will of the individual, and good balance with the second phalange is of great significance. A long first section and a short-changed second one would indicate that the person's will is not guided by good judgment or reasoning but only by "want." A comparatively short thumb tip and much longer second section has the opposite effect; i.e., the individual reveals the inability to make quick decisions, thus he may be missing many opportunities in his life.

The Palm: (See Map of the Palm, Figure 35)

The section of the palm that refers to the mentality of the person is the "Quadrangle," situated between the lines of Heart and Head. As the palm can also be divided vertically, the area between Jupiter and Saturn is the conscious sphere, where the mental/objective activities are registered. The space between the middle of the Saturn finger and Mercury lies in the subconscious zone that I call the "mental/creative" sphere. Although a person is unaware of it, brain waves function continuously, and it is often through these subconscious mental activities that one receives the solution to problems that the active mind has been unable to find.

In the Handwriting: (Figure 151)

The three zones in the handwriting were discussed in PART III, Chapter 13. If the upper is well-developed in height or width or in good balance with the middle and lower zones, such a person is goal-oriented and his mentality is directed toward fulfilling those desires, the nature of which will be determined by the rest of his writing.

The signature in Figure 151 exemplifies a flair for drama and music or dance, and although the upper zone is greatly exaggerated, it is balanced by the same length and fullness in the lower zone, which points to Victoria Principal's perceptive talent in that direction. The well-defined middle zone, with its regularity and even base line, suggests that her talent is also balanced by practical goals, and that she has both feet planted on the ground.

- An upper zone that extends little beyond the middle zone shows a lack of goals due to laziness or complacency; it may also be due to a lack of energy, in which case the writing would have a light pressure.
- Enrolled strokes in the upper zone show egotism and possessiveness, and exaggerated embellishments reveal that the individual attaches importance to petty details, while missing the larger and more important issues. He or she are also concerned with appearances.
- A tall but lean or simplified upper zone, created by the omission of loops, indicates analytical, abstract thinking and a keen intellect and mentality.
- Originality in letter formations in the upper zone are an expression of creative perception, or an indication of dramatic instincts which translates into showmanship that is not restricted to the acting profession, but is often present, as demonstrated by the signatures of Victoria Principal and Jane Seymour, Figures 151 and 136 respectively.

To give optimum value to a tall upper zone, it must be supported by a well-balanced lower and a legible middle zone, with a moderately even base line and regular writing, otherwise the high ideas reflected by the tall or full upper zone may result in mere "pipe dreams."

THE SOCIAL/EMOTIONAL ZONE
The Hand:

The second phalanges of the fingers and thumb indicate how the ideas perceived from the outside and from within us are being utilized. As already discussed, each finger and thumb represent different areas of functioning.

- The second phalange of the Jupiter finger indicates executive abilities and planning, provided that the finger is of at least average length. All three finger sections should be of roughly equal length to be considered average.
- The second section of the Saturn finger relates to the application of knowledge pertaining to science and law; a full second section also shows love of agriculture and "mother earth," which I can readily confirm!
- The Apollo finger: if this section is well-developed, it indicates good visual and color sense, provided that the finger itself is of at least average length.
- The second section of the Mercury finger reflects how well the ideas in business, science or music are being utilized. For optimum value, the finger should be of at least average length.
- The Thumb: this section measures logic and reasoning if in proper balance with the thumb tip.

The Palm:

The section of the palm pertaining to the emotions is from the base of the fingers to the Heart line, and it also includes the "Girdle of Venus." (PART II, Chapter 8). Half of this section, from the fingers of Jupiter to the middle of Saturn, lies in the conscious zone, whereas the section from that point to Mercury and to the edge of the palm, called "percussion," is designated to the unconscious. The functions ascribed to that portion of the hand are, therefore, subject to our automatic and instinctive functioning.

The absence of a dividing line between the mental/emotional and the mental/objective zone, as is the case when the "Simian" line is present, (PART II, Chapter 7), can result in lack of objectivity. Other deviations may affect this as well, such as the Heart line lying too low in the palm and encroaching on the Head line, or the opposite, where the Head line takes over the space destined for the Heart line. The latter would describe someone whose rationalizations would always take the upper hand over his emotions.

The Handwriting:

The middle zone (PART III, Chapter 13) is clearly the most important one, as it reflects our conscious daily functioning. Although it is influenced by the perceptions registered in the upper zone, and by the subconscious, instinctive desires and needs expressed in the lower zone, the middle zone reveals our "modus operandi."

The bottom of the lowercase letters is the base line, which may be compared to the ground we walk on. If even and moderately regular, it indicates that we have control over our life, and that we are not aimlessly driven by moods of elation or depression. If letters do not return to the base line but are suspended in the air, it reflects inhibition or uncertainty. If final letters or ending strokes are pressed below the base line, it may be a sign of suppression or discouragement, especially if made with light pressure. If heavy pressure is applied, such "dragged down" ending strokes manifest strong, inflexible convictions and emotional release, which can result in fits of temper.

Some letters take in more than one zone, such as f, h, l and t; only the "f" encompasses all three zones. If well-balanced, it gives a clue to the writer's flexibility in adjusting to different situations.

The all-important personal pronoun "I", called PPI, and other capital letters take in the middle and upper zones.

- If the PPI is larger than the other capital letters, it reveals an exaggerated self-esteem.
- Same size PPI as other capitals reflects a healthy ego, which is neither over nor understated.
- Where the PPI is written in a lowercase "i", or if smaller and more left-slanted than the other capital letters, it reveals a low self-esteem.
- A vertical PPI in vertical writing indicates poise and self-reliance.
- A left-slanted PPI in left-slanted writing expresses self-centered ego involvement, while a left-slanted PPI coupled with a

right slant writing gives a clue to inhibition of a personal nature while outwardly social.

- Large, embellished or ostentatious capital letters are a desire for showmanship or power. The latter displays vulgar tastes.
- A large middle zone with upper and lower zones extending very little above or below the base line may show a lack of goals or energy, or it may reveal a phlegmatic nature.
- Fluctuating height of the middle zone goes hand in hand with uncertainty or emotional instability, especially if coupled with a change in the slant.

THE PHYSICAL/INSTINCTUAL ZONE
The Hand:

The third section of the fingers relate to our physical/instinctual being, and pertain to our physical and sensual needs.

- The Jupiter finger: if the third section dominates over the other two, it indicates a tendency toward physical appetites. In a more "intellectual" hand, this could reveal personal charisma. A puffy third section is an indication of self-indulgence in one area or another.
- The Saturn finger: this section relates to the stability of the home; if this phalange dominates, it shows a clear preference toward traditional values.
- The Apollo finger: if the third phalange is well-developed, it shows discrimination in food, dress or furnishings, but it should not be fat or puffy, as this would reveal a preference for quantity over quality.
- The Mercury finger: the third section shows independence in love if at least average length; this is enhanced if Mercury leans away from the Apollo finger.

The Palm:

The entire lower section of the palm, separated by the imaginary line from the onset of the thumb to the wrist section, lies in the unconscious zone, (Figure 150), and is designated to our physical/instinctual needs and appetites. One section where these can be measured is the

Mount of Venus, encircled by the Life line, which is also the third section of the thumb. If this mount is well-padded but firm, it gives evidence of a healthy interest in sexuality and personal warmth, but if exaggerated in development or soft and flabby, such a person will most likely be at the mercy of his own impulses rather than in control of them.

The seat of our deepest unconscious is the Mount of Luna, which can be compared with the ID - the nucleus of our personality. It is also the center from which our creative imagination arises. A well-developed Mount of Luna should, therefore, be accompanied by other signs of creativity or originality in the hand, such as: a long finger and developed Mount of Apollo; lines beneath Apollo; Head line curving slightly toward the Mount of Luna; edge of palm, "percussion" well-developed and bulging outward.

The Handwriting:

The space below the base line is called the unconscious sphere. It represents our instinctual and physical needs. Full lower zone loops that dip down into the "unawareness" and complete their journey by resurfacing to the base line into our "awareness" show joy of life and vitality. Exaggerated loops in fullness or length reflect above normal needs for sensual or material gratification. Still, by returning to the base line, the writer is dealing with these needs in one way or another, while loops or single strokes that stay below the base line show the writer's suppression of his desires.

- Ineffectual lower zones that extend very little below the base line may indicate a lack of energy, or neglect of physical/sensual activity.
- Lower zone loops or strokes without pressure show diminished energy, or uncertainty, especially if executed in a wavy or jittery fashion.
- Lower zone loops or single strokes with pressure reveal energy, vitality and concentration.
- Extended, long and/or full lower zone: above average sexual activity or materialistic needs.

- Irregularities in the lower zone, such as different kinds of lower zone loops in one writing, reveal peculiarities which may point to unusual sexual habits or a lack of sexual identity, which, in some cases, may give a clue to homosexuality.
- Good proportion in height and fullness of the three zones gives evidence of emotional maturity, enjoyment of life and harmonious functioning, as well as flexibility and the ability to make adjustments.

CONCLUSIONS

As the zonal distribution in the hand and in handwriting varies from one person to another, it enhances the individuality of man. How these three zones work and interrelate with each other can give you valuable insight into your own and other personalities.

I encourage you to have pen and paper handy while examining these zonal proportions, in order to see for yourself how and if they bond and interface with each other.

Just as some people are easier to get to "know," you will find some hands and writings easier to "read," which expresses the vast variation in complexity and/or versatility among human beings.

Figure 151, The Division in the Handwriting

U-Zone:	Goals, Imagination, Perception
M-Zone:	Realism, Day-by Day Functioning
L-Zone:	Sensuality, Physical Materialistic Needs

Figure 150, The Division in the Palm and Fingers

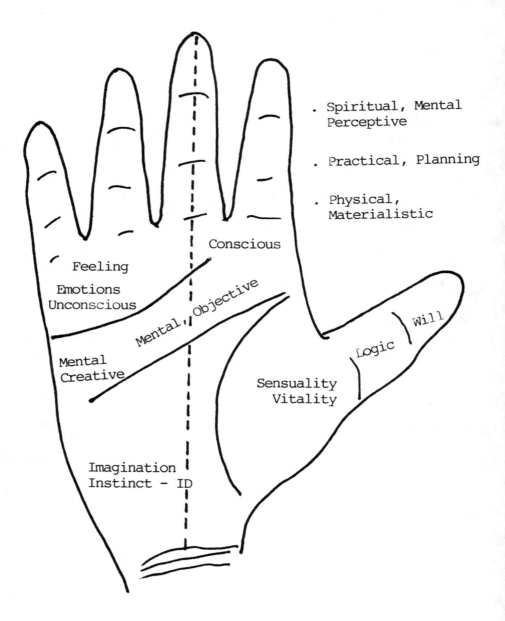

25

The Interrelation of the Hand and Writing

CORRESPONDING ATTITUDES AND CHARACTERISTICS

Not ALL the signs have to be present in one hand or writing.

SIGNS IN THE HAND

SIGNS IN THE HANDWRITING

Adaptable

Flexible thumb and fingers; existence of Fate line; long nails; tendency for the Jupiter finger to lean toward the Saturn finger.

Figure 8 "g"s, fluency in writing; garland or mixed connections; moderately connected writing; no wide spaces between words.

Adventurous

Life line forming wide circle around ball of the thumb (Mount of Venus;) branch of Life line veering toward the Mount of Luna; fingers spread widely when held up in the air.

Wide horizontal expansion in writing; right margin of the page smaller than left; different kinds of letter formations for one letter; generous usage of space.

Aggressive

The two Mounts of Mars, especially the Mount of Lower Mars (Figure 34) well-developed; full and heavy finger and thumb tips; nails shorter than long.

Angle connections; downward slanted "t"-bars and "i"-dots; heavy pressure; pointed dagger-strokes and hooks.

SIGNS IN THE HAND | SIGNS IN THE HANDWRITING

Affectionate

Mount of Venus well-developed; Heart line strong; starting from beneath fingers of Jupiter or in-between Jupiter and Saturn.

Mostly garland connections; full writing, including loop formations; ending strokes to the right.

Ambitious

Lines on Mount of Jupiter, or branch from Fate line to Jupiter, or branch from Head line toward Jupiter; long, well-developed Jupiter finger; same applies to the Mount; Finger of Jupiter leaning toward thumb.

Rising base line; "t"-bars crossed high on the stem, or rising upward; highly dotted, or slashed "i"-dots; pressure medium to heavy; tall upper zone.

Analytical

Long Head line, straight or only slightly curving toward the Mount of Luna; top phalange of fingers and both sections of thumb long and well-balanced; long thumbs.

Tops of lowercase letters angular, such as in "m"s and "n"s; tendency toward simplification in writing; connected writing or print script.

Cautious/Fearful

Life line starting from within the Head line or running together for a distance; Life line making narrow circle around the Mount of Venus; tendency of the fingers to cling together when holding up in the air.

Small left margin, usually smaller than right; not using all the available space; writing compressed rather than full; ending strokes often turning leftward; slant may be left, vertical or right, but usually tendency toward left is prevalent.

Creative

Head line curving gently toward the Mount of Luna; Head line may have fork toward Mount of Luna; Apollo finger at least average length; lines on Mount of Apollo; edge of palm (Percussion) well-rounded.

Originality of letter formations; presence of varied letter formations for one letter; "i"-dots highly placed; mixed connections, i.e., garlands, angles, arcades, thread; printed capital letters.

SIGNS IN THE HAND	SIGNS IN THE HANDWRITING
Dependable	
Strong major lines; firm Saturn finger; line of Heart starting from beneath Jupiter or between Jupiter and Saturn fingers; good line of Heart; good spacing between the lines of Heart and Head.	Moderately regular writing; legible. Even base line; not much change of slant; good spacing between words and lines; signature may be congruent with text of writing, but it should be similar in style with the text.
Domineering	
Very long Jupiter finger, longer than Apollo finger; fingertip of Mercury may also be long, showing persuasiveness; exaggerated development in Mount of Jupiter.	Prominent upper-zone strokes, sharp and pointed; "t"-bars very high, with pressure; tendency to find slashing strokes, heavy periods and ending strokes. Angular connections.
Dynamic	
Texture of palm and fingers elastic and firm; well-developed Mounts of Venus, Luna. Color of skin pink, and major lines well-marked; fingers spread widely when held in the air, with a tendency to lean toward the thumb.	Prominent upper-zone, leaning toward the right; "t"-bars and "i"-dots placed high and to the right of the letter; spontaneous writing; small right margin and generous usage of writing space; PPI (Personal Pronoun I) should not be small.
Energetic	
Firm texture of hands and fingers; color of skin should be pink; major lines well-marked; color of nails should also be pink. Well-developed mounts.	Medium to heavy pressure in writing; also medium to fast writing with tendency toward movements to the right; good balance in the three zones.

SIGNS IN THE HAND	SIGNS IN THE HANDWRITING

Even-tempered

Rounded fingertips; longer finger nails than wide; palm rounded at the base of the fingers; major lines well-marked and of pink color as well as the skin of the palm.	Mostly garland connections; pressure of writing light to medium; good rightward ending strokes; slant of writing moderately even; legible, rhythmic writing without "jerky" strokes.

Extroverted

Life line in wide circle around the Mount of Venus with well-developed mount; fingers spread widely when held up in the air; social sphere between base of fingers to line of Heart well-developed; may have a "Girdle of Venus;" Heart line starting from beneath Jupiter or between Jupiter and Saturn fingers.	Wide and predominantly full writing; word and line spacing not too wide; ending strokes to the right; generous usage of the available space; pasty rather than sharp writing; small right margin.

Explosive-Hot Temper

Major lines in palm and finger nails red; finger nails may be broader than long; thumb tips heavy and bulbous; the lines of Heart and Head may be shorter than average, but this may not be the case; texture of palm and fingers coarse; well-developed Mount of Lower Mars.	Hooks and daggers in writing; sudden pressure; slashed "t"-bars and "i"-dots with pressure heavier at the ending point; blunt or no ending strokes; heavy final strokes; writing may be "pasty," at least in places; angular connections.

Fast-Thinking

Tapered fingertips; long first sections of fingers and thumbs; long Head line.	Good speed in writing; natural writing; "t"-bars and "i"-dots crossed to the right; mixture of connections; horizontal expansion.

SIGNS IN THE HAND	SIGNS IN THE HANDWRITING

Flexible

Fingers and thumbs bend back easily; if exaggerated, they bend back like india rubber, which is the extreme; loop patterns on fingertips; fine-textured skin rather than coarse.	Garland, thread or double-curve connections; light to medium pressure; good rhythm; if thread or double-curve dominate, rhythm may become slack, which is negative.

Signs of Frustration

Horizontal lines on the Mount of Venus touching or cutting Life line; horizontal lines on the Mount of Luna; hollow interior of palm; network of fine lines crossing the palm.	Constricted, narrow writing; sudden pressure; irregularity in writing, in slant, size of middle zone; ending strokes descending below base line.

Introverted

Life line starting from WITHIN the Head line, proceeding in a narrow circle around the thumb; Mount of Venus not well-developed; fleshless hand; quite often hollow palm; other mounts may or may not be well-developed either.	Narrow writing; often left slant or trend; large spacing between words; right margin wider than left; small writing with arcade or angular connections prevalent.

Independent

Separation of the Life and Head lines at the beginning; line of Fate starting from the wrist not touching the Life line; fingers spread widely when hand is held up in the air; Jupiter finger leaning toward the thumb, and Mercury finger spaced away from Apollo; good space between the Head and Heart lines. (Quadrangle)	Few or no lead-in strokes to capital and small-case letters; good word and line spacing, not touching or interfering with each other; firm pressure; no exaggerated embellishments; there may be varied forms of connections, and/ or signs of originality, not copybook writing.

SIGNS IN THE HAND	SIGNS IN THE HANDWRITING

Signs of Insincerity

A crooked finger of Mercury, or other twisted fingers, or overlapping each other; irregularities in the placement of the Head and/or Heart line, either one or the other encroaching on their respective space.

Much retracing and mending of letters, or adding strokes after they are written; illegible writing; "a"s and "o"s open at the bottom instead of the top; missing letters; mixture of writing styles in one sample.

Jealousy

The Heart line lying straight across the palm from Mercury to Jupiter, reveals too great a dependence on affections; line of Heart may be too close to Head line.

Small, circle, or enrolled formations at the beginning or inside the letters; rolled-in or retraced loops. It is important to observe in which way they occur.

Signs of Leadership

Strong Jupiter finger of at least average length; Mount of Jupiter well-developed; branch from Fate line toward Jupiter; texture of hand should be fleshy but firm, rather than thin and bony; if the latter applies, along with the above prerequisites, it could indicate leadership on the religious or intellectual plane; possession of a strong thumb.

Moderately large writing, if leadership in politics, etc.; if moderately small writing leadership will be on intellectual plane; word spacing should be sufficient, but not too wide; right slant with high "t"-bars; medium to heavy pressure; good individual rhythm; few lead-in strokes to capital and lowercase letters.

Nervous Disposition

A cold, clammy hand and sweaty palm; a network of fine lines criss-crossing the palm; covering of fingers when talking, or tucking the thumb inside the palm.

Tremor in writing; much retracing or mending of letters; pressure is either very light or sporadic; break-down of letter formation; wavy base line; irregularity in writing.

SIGNS IN THE HAND	SIGNS IN THE HANDWRITING

Objective

The space between the Head and Heart lines, called the Quadrangle, should not be too narrow, or the lines should not interfere with one another; when the Head and Heart lines run together as one (Simian line) it shows lack of objectivity in some area.

Adequate line spacing; i.e., lines not interfering with one another, should not be too wide; clear word spacing; no extreme loop formations.

Practical

The course of the Head line should be on the straight side; square-type palm and fingers, but this hand can have a mixture of other types of fingers, such as spatulate or rounded.

Good zonal balance in writing, i.e., upper middle, lower zones not extremely unbalanced; a "no-frill" type of writing with few embellishments.

Perceptive

May possess an intuition line; tapered fingertips; line of Head curving gently toward the Mount of Luna; other mounts such as Jupiter, Apollo and Mercury well-developed.

Tall upper zone, with or without loops, not exaggerated; some disconnections in an otherwise moderately connected writing; mixed connections; i.e., garlands, arcades, angles, thread.

Philosophic

Fingers may be long, but not necessarily; top finger joints knotty or well-marked; Head line curving toward Mount of Luna; presence of Fate line; fingertips rounded or tapered rather than square; fingernails longer than broad.

Emphasis on upper zone; simplifications prevalent; may have Greek letter formations, i.e., d, e, g, h, k, l; mixed connections; aesthetic writing.

SIGNS IN THE HAND	SIGNS IN THE HANDWRITING

Persistent

Strong thumbs of at least average length; major lines well-marked; texture of palm and fingers firm; strong handshake.	Moderately regular writing with medium to heavy pressure; hooks or "ties" and "knots" such as in "t"s; final strokes to the right.

Persuasive

Well-developed Jupiter finger; long fingertip in Mercury finger; this finger may lean toward Apollo, emphasizing persuasion; when held up in the air, fingers have tendency to lean toward the thumb; well-developed mounts of Jupiter, Mercury.	"t"-bars firm and extended to the right of the letter; predominant right slant; small right margin; medium to heavy pressure; word spacing should be sufficient and not too wide.

Self-Confident

Texture of hands and palm elastic and firm; strong handshake; fingers separated when held up in the air; Jupiter and Mercury fingers should not be set low on the palm; major lines well-marked.	Natural, spontaneous writing with good rhythm; PPI will neither be too small nor too large; average size capital letters; good zonal balance.

Slow Thinking

Heavy-textured or coarse hand; may also have thick fingers, square-tipped rather than tapered; Head line straight and not too long.	Careful, laborious writing; tops of "m"s and "n"s rounded, not pointed; carefully placed "t"-bars and "i"-dots; heavy period; no elegant connective strokes.

Sensuous

Exaggerated development of Mount of Venus and/or Luna; base sections of fingers and thumbs may be soft and puffy; lower half of palm well-developed; line of Heart may end under the Mount of Saturn.	Flooded ovals in lowercase letters; smeary or "pastose" ductus; long lower zone, with or without loops, often causing interference with the lines below; eccentric loop formations in lower zone.

SIGNS IN THE HAND	SIGNS IN THE HANDWRITING

Sincere/Honest

Fingers straight and firm when hand is held up in the air; no crooked fingers; well-developed Heart line, which should not interfere with Head line; well-marked major lines; few horizontal lines crossing the palm; no crooked or overlapping fingers.

Legible script; not much retracing; Signature similar in style and size with text; there should not be different styles of writing within one sample, such as mixture of cursive and print, or different types of print script; clear word and line spacing; no extreme embellishments or enrollments.

Sociable

Mounts of Venus and other mounts well-developed; line of Life forms wide circle around thumb; handtype: conic/artistic; i.e., rounded or tapered fingers and tips, especially the Apollo finger; palm should not be bony and thin; or hollow center.

Rounded letter formations; mixed connections; horizontal expansion in writing rather than tightly squeezed; small right margin; ending strokes continue to the right, predominantly right slant of writing; if vertical or left slant writing should be full; word spacing and right margin not wide.

Stubborn/Unyielding

Stiff, inflexible thumbs and fingers; short nails, often found in the hands of the square and spatulate type; square-tipped rather than tapered finger and thumb tips.

Angular writing; stubborn "t"-bars, (PART III - Chapter 19); blunt or few ending strokes to the right; final movement of letters descending below the base line, with pressure.

Sympathetic/Warmhearted

Well-developed Mount of Venus; lively, full-fleshed hand, but firm, not puffy; line of Heart long, ending under Jupiter or between Jupiter and Saturn fingers; rounded palm on base of fingers.

Ending strokes to the right; garland connections prevail, or with mixed connectives; good rhythm in writing; full, rather than meager and squeezed writing.

SIGNS IN THE HAND   SIGNS IN THE HANDWRITING

Temper, Signs of

Bulbous or heavy thumb and finger tips; short fingers without developed joints indicate quickness to lose temper; color of major lines in palm, as well as of the fingernails, is deep red rather than pink; fingernails shorter than long.

"t"-bars and "i"-dots are slashes and often heavier at the ending point, resembling a club; if heavier at the onset of the "t"-bar it indicates aggression in the form of sarcasm; "temper-tics," which are small hooks on beginning and ending strokes; heavy or sudden pressure.

Vital/Energetic

Color of fingernails and lines pink; well-marked major lines, especially Life line; well-padded Mount of Venus and other mounts; texture of hand and fingers firm but elastic.

Pressure of writing medium to heavy; moderate speed; narrow right margin; "t"-bars and "i"-dots to the right of the stem; ascending words and lines.

Versatile

Well-developed and marked Head line, which may be curving gently toward the Mount of Luna; Head line may be forked toward Mounts of Luna or Mercury; variety of fingertips; i.e., square or conic/tapered; mixture of fingertip patterns; i.e., loop whorl, arch patterns.

Variations in letter formations; signs of originality in letter formations; mixture of connections; tying-in of "i"-dots or of "t"-bars with next or previous letters; different kinds of letter formations for one writing sample; fluency of individual rhythm; moderately fast writing.

26

The Practical
Personality Types

General Procedures in Hand and Handwriting Analysis

IN PERSON, I WOULD EXAMINE BOTH HANDS OF THE INDIVIDUAL TO COMPARE them with regard to changes that may have taken place in the development from the left, or "birth," to the right, or "dominant" hand, assuming that the person is right-handed. In this book, for our purposes, we will evaluate the right hand only, since it is the "now" hand and should therefore correlate best with the findings in the handwriting. It is an excellent idea to record the data on a check sheet.

It is not my aim to render a detailed analysis of the hands as well as the corresponding handwritings, but rather to establish the basic "modus operandi" of the individual.

The following chapters show a cross-section of all types of hands/ handwritings, ranging in age from young to middle age and beyond.

THE PRACTICAL/USEFUL PERSONALITY

This handprint and handwriting (HP 3 A - HW 3 A-A) belong to a male of about 55. The hand is large, but considering that he is over six feet tall with a rangy build, it is not out of proportion. The hand comes closest to the pure "Practical/Useful" type (PART I - Chapter 1).

The hand is characterized by a large, square and heavy palm and short fingers, set squarely on the palm. This shows that this man loves action and reaction, with the resulting "short fuse" in discharging his feelings of anger, frustration or pleasure, as they occur. The squareness of the palm shows his ability to convert knowledge about a subject into practical solutions, which he will do efficiently and with expediency, for he does not believe in wasting time on non-essentials. A strong will and determination necessary to carry out his goals and needs are also revealed in the thick but rather inflexible thumb, which indicates that once he is on a set course of action, he does not readily want to change it.

The handwriting confirms the above findings in the following area: It is matter-of-fact, void of additional strokes and flourishes, indicating his love of facts and figures, yet it is clear and legible. That he is a man-of-action is seen in the right-ward slant, and the strong "t"-bars, some of which are executed with heavy pressure and additional hooks and dashes, confirming his immediate reactions to stimuli. These contrast with his otherwise deliberate writing. The hooks further indicate a desire to hold onto things he considers his possessions, which may be on a material or emotional plane.

This man's practical intelligence is further reflected in the straight and clearly marked Head line. The other two major lines of Life and Heart are also well-defined. Such a person is not a "star-gazer;" he has down-to-earth needs and goals, which he pursues with a single-mindedness of purpose. He is materialistic in a sense that he possesses solid, primary needs, such as the stability of home, family, etc., and his sense of practicality would far outweigh any aesthetic consideration. The well-developed mounts or elevations on his palmar surface, especially the Mount of Venus, indicate a healthy appetite for the physical/sensual. The mounts of Upper and Lower Mars are also well-padded, which reveals a "fighting spirit." Lower Mars is situated just above the insertion of the thumb, while Upper Mars lies across the palm on the percussion-side of the hand, which is bulging slightly. (See PART I - Chapter 6). If a fighting spirit is channeled into creative and constructive endeavors, it shows determination and endurance. Such a person does not give up easily in anything he feels strongly about.

In the handwriting, this is confirmed in the deliberate, plodding movement of his script. This shows a strong resolve also
seen in the heavy pressure of the "t"s. Some tops of small letter
"n"s are pointed, which reveal his analytical, practical mind.
This is further expressed in the connected writing, reflecting a
logical train of thought and follow-through. The well-balanced
proportions of the upper, middle and lower zones give further
evidence or realistic goals. The presence of a tenacious fighting
spirit are the small hooks and tics, which are primarily present
in the "t"-crossings.

This man has an emotional side as well, but finds it hard to express his feelings. As the Earth appears calm and motionless on the
surface, it may be seething like a cauldron beneath the earth's crust,
which shows its duality also in the personality. In the hand, this
emotional side is evidenced by the large space from the base of the
fingers to the Heart line, whereas the distance between the Heart and
Head lines, called the "Quadrangle," is proportionally narrower, revealing a somewhat dogmatic disposition which can result in a lack of
tolerance and understanding. He sees things in terms of black-and-
white or right-or-wrong. From the good zonal balance in the hands,
fingers, thumb and phalanges, it is evident that this man possesses
many of the strong, solid qualities ascribed to the practical/useful personality type.

In the handwriting, the need for material and sensual gratification is revealed in the occasional long and full lower-zone
loops, which interfere very slightly with the lines below. It does
not seem to affect his daily functioning, since the middle zone is
clearly spaced with a regular and even base line.

His sensitivity to criticism is seen in looped "d"s and "t"s,
which indicates his vulnerability. He needs to protect a very
strong masculine image, and he would interpret any criticism as
undermining it. The lack of subtleness or tact is revealed in
blunt ending strokes of letters, (PART III - Chapter 18), an
indication that he is used to communicating with people in a
matter-of-fact manner.

CAREER APTITUDES

This person would do well in any work situation where he can put his practical abilities and logical thinking to good use. He is not a natural scholar or theoretician, but he is a master at putting his knowledge into practice. He will excel in a "hands-on" type of career in any practical/technical field. It is essential that he be mentally as well as physically active. The latter is very important since this type of person is able to discharge many frustrations in a constructive fashion; otherwise they might erupt like a volcanic explosion. Judging from his strong index/Jupiter finger and thumb, this man can handle people and responsibilities.

(This man is a building foreman.)

Figure HW 3 A-A, The Practical Personality Type

How many years do you e before you start withdraw As a quick look at the acco chart indicates; the earni IRA accelerate over time — constant rate of return — longer the money remains better the account looks.

Figure HP 3, A

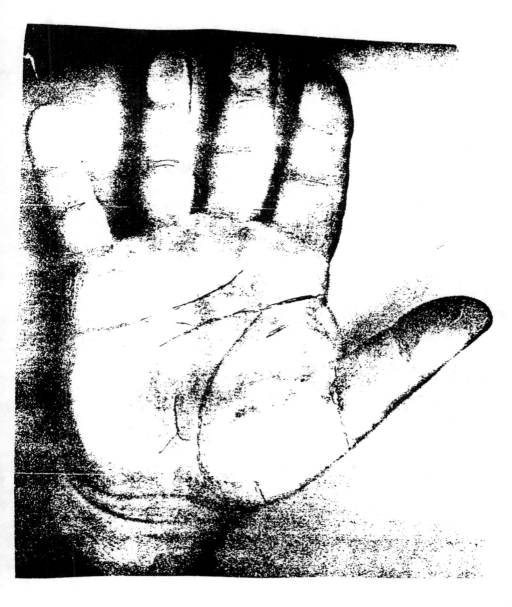

THE PRACTICAL/MANAGERIAL PERSONALITY

This handprint and handwriting (HP 3 B - HW 3 B-B) belong to a female, about 48 years old. The hand resembles the previous one only in its relative squareness, but has a slightly longer palm compared to its width. The hand is a combination of the Practical/Earth, and the Intellectual/Air types; it has retained the practicality of the former, adding a new dimension with the latter hand type. The long fingers and stronger flexibility suggest more patience with details, and a love of study for its own sake. Long fingers are also a built-in control valve for the emotions which are expressed with greater tact and verbal skills than if the owner of this hand were the pure Practical/Useful type. The influence of the Intellectual type further suggests good communication skills and a high regard for order in all things.

The fingertips vary in shape from rounded to slightly tapered. Jupiter and the thumb are the most tapered, indicating quickness in perceptions, while Apollo's rounded fingertip reveals sociability and understanding. Saturn's tip is the most square, which gives a clue to a practical business sense and an appreciation of the stability of home, and adherence to traditional values. This is confirmed by the firm base of the thumb, the tip of which is more flexible, indicating flexibility of ideas.

In the handwriting, versatility is reflected in the moderately fast writing and in the mixture of letter formations, which vary from simplified/abstracted to the copy-book style. This explains that while this person is very much interested and active in career and worldly activities, she also possesses very definite sets of values and probably adheres to traditions religiously. This is further confirmed in some of the tent-shaped "t"s, which are referred to as the "stubborn t's," (PART III - Chapter 19). It signifies that if she feels strongly about something, she is not apt to change her mind. This duality of flexibility and inflexibility is also evidenced in the fluid flow of her writing, coupled with straight and stiff lead-in strokes, which are primarily seen in lowercase letters.

The major lines of Life, Head and Heart are clearly imprinted on the palmar surface, but there are also a network of fine lines crisscrossing it, which point to the sensitivity of a highly developed nervous system. The Life line, though strong in parts, reveals some horizontal bars or obstacles which indicate that her level of energy and vitality is not always consistent, and that she would do well to preserve these well. The Head line is slightly separated from the Life line at its inception, which shows independence and leadership potential. The Head line, while on a straight course at the beginning, curves toward the Mount of Luna on the second half of the palm, attesting not only to the practical abilities but to her imagination, either as an appreciator of beauty in nature, etc., or as a practicing artist.

From her Heart line, which starts on the Mount of Jupiter, loyalty and dependability in her affections are clearly indicated. The danger exists that she would put those she loves on a pedestal, with resulting disappointments later on.

The space between the Heart and Head lines, called the "Quadrangle," is wide, suggesting fairness and tolerance. The presence of the two Fate lines, one starting from the wrist and the other halfway up in the palm, reflects this person's strong sets of values and efforts toward continuous growth as a human being.

In the writing, her practical, logical intelligence is revealed in the highly connected writing, indicating a logical train of thought. While some of the lowercase letters are distinctly formed, the tops of "n"s and "u"s express quick perceptions. The presence of threaded connections reveal that, while she is fully capable of paying excellent attention to details, she can also bypass them when she has to deal with larger issues. This is also reflected in the excellent word and line spacing, which shows organizational skills and objectivity.

The right margin of the writing is smaller than the left which signifies that she is interested in people and takes an active part in worldly affairs. Optimism is revealed in the rising lines of her writing.

CAREER APTITUDES

This person's current position as office manager and computer programmer lets her use her excellent managerial abilities and well-functioning intelligence. She is definitely qualified for leadership; whether she desires its burden and responsibility depends on her. This question mark is indicated in her index finger which is shorter than the Apollo finger.

Her capabilities would be an asset in the teaching profession as well, for she has the necessary prerequisites; i.e., intelligence, patience and tolerance.

Figure HW 3, B-B, The Practical/Managerial Personality

Figure HP 3, B, The Practical/Managerial Personality

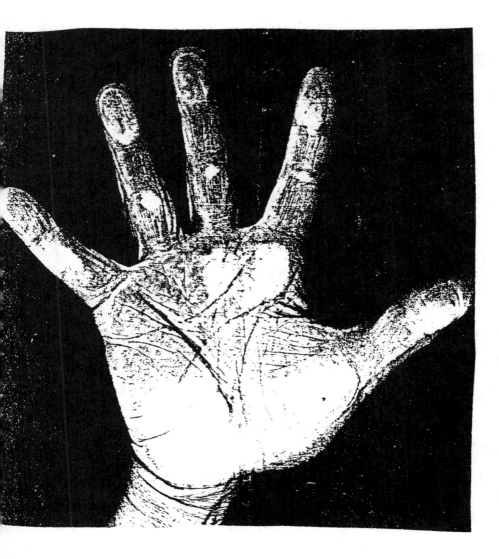

27

The Intellectual Personality

THE TWO HANDPRINTS AND HANDWRITINGS SHOW MANY SIMILARITIES AND DIS-similarities, because they are combined with different "sub-types." The man's hand is a combination of the Intellectual and the Spatulate/Energetic hand type, while the woman's hand correlates the Intellectual with the Artistic/Aesthetic type.

As the Intellectual type is an "evolved Earth type," it is distinguished chirognomically by a squarish palm and long fingers, finer skin texture and additional lines on the palmar surface. The masculine hand is moderately large with full fingers, often with pronounced joints, which reveal a philosophic outlook. The female counterpart is smaller in size, although not an extremely small hand, with fingers that vary from the thin to the more fleshed-out variety.

The Intellectual hand type reflects the Air-Element, which generally has a built-in facility for expression and intellectual flexibility. This translates into versatility on an intellectual basis. Another native characteristic of this hand type is the desire for order and organization in thought processes relating to their lives. If this expands to career or politics, such a person expects the same capacity from others, which rarely happens, since the majority of people do not possess the same high intellectual standards.

Another characteristic inherent to this personality type is patience and deliberation; such individuals do not usually make rash decisions. The long fingers stem the flow of rashness and impulse.

The Intellectual/Air type has the tendency to rationalize his emotions and to suppress them if they get in the way of his intellect.

THE INTELLECTUAL/INNOVATIVE PERSONALITY

The handprint and handwriting belong to a male, past 70, a retired scientist, (HP 4 A - HW 4 A-A). This hand is a combination of at least two major types, i.e., the Intellectual/Philosophic and the Spatulate/Energetic. The influence of the latter is seen in the slightly triangular formation of the lower part of the palm, and in the spatulate fingertips of the Apollo Mercury fingers. (PART I - Chapters 1 and 3).

The Spatulate is the most innovative and individualistic of all the hand types, which is further reflected in the "whorl" pattern of the thumb, Saturn and Apollo fingers. Mercury and Jupiter have loop formations, indicating adaptability and flexibility. (PART II - Chapter 8). The "whorl" pattern signifies individuality, which is a positive characteristic if coupled with other favorable signs, such as a strong thumb and a straight, unwavering Head line, which are present in this hand.

The well-developed mounts, especially the Mount of Luna, which is the seat of creative imagination, indicate vitality and physical and mental energy.

In the handwriting, above average intelligence is seen in the simplified and abstracted writing, (PART III - Chapter 14), which is indicative of a person who gets to the heart of the matter without wasting time on unnecessary details. He has the patience for details if they are of interest to him.

His writing is primarily "disconnected;" i.e., fewer than five letters are conjoined without interruptions; this reflects the presence of intuition, allowing an influx of creative ideas to enter his mind. The forms of connectives themselves are a mixture of garlands, arcades and threads, and angles are seen in some of the pointed tops of lowercase "n"s, "u"s, etc., which indicates a discerning and analytical mind. The writing at this stage is not showing the dynamic energy that the hand still reflects, which may be the result of a general slowing-down process.

The major lines in the hand are clearly marked and well-positioned. The slight separation of the lines of Head and Life at their starting points is an indication that such a person is not bound to tradition and conventions, confirming that he takes the novel approach to things, which is an inherent characteristic of the Spatulate hand type. The Head line suggests both practical and analytical abilities, while the Heart line expresses loyalty in his affections. The line of Life encircles the ball of the thumb in a wide path, reflecting a spirit of adventure and a "wide horizon;" the deep, strong line shows uninterrupted vitality and is a sign of robust good health. The presence of a Fate line with a starting point near the wrist confirms early independence; this line continues upward into the palm toward its destination, the Mount of Saturn, which suggests unwavering efforts for self-actualization. The lines beneath the Apollo finger indicate a variety of interests that started rather late in this person's life.

From his writing, creativity and imagination are seen in printed capital letters and in some of the highly placed "i"-dots. Since the "i"s are not always dotted, it indicates a "selective memory," or it could be a reflection of forgetfulness in some areas.

The small, vertical writing also indicates good concentration. The wide word and line spacing also suggest that he does not have the need for constant contact with others, preferring to immerse himself in projects, studies, etc. This person is socially adept, however. He possesses poise and tact and has a gentle, non-aggressive disposition, which is indicated in some of the rounded letter formations, and the absence of angularity in the connections. The wide line spacing further enhances his individuality and intellectual detachment.

CAREER APTITUDES

This man's above average intelligence and discerning mind will find new avenues, or improve existing ones, which would be excellent assets in pioneering research in any field of interest to him. His full hands and fingers suggest that he would like variety on mental and physical planes. Such desires could be combined in careers such as oceanography, archeology, geology, etc., where he could satisfy his physical and mental energy. Such professions would provide stimuli and versatility, because routine or monotonous work would not be to his liking.

(This man is a retired physicist.)

Figure HW 4 A-A, The Innovative Personality

*Here are a few lines of handwriting &
the palm prints. I hope you find th
meaningful and useful in your analys*

Figure HP 4, A, The Innovative Personality

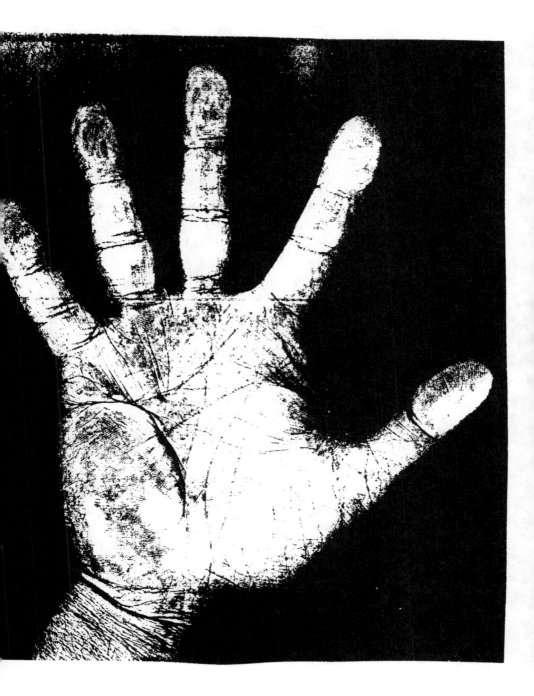

THE INTELLECTUAL/AESTHETIC PERSONALITY

The handprint and two variations of handwriting belong to a female, about 54, (HP 4 B - HW 4 B-B).

The hand is of average size compared to her body build, and its characteristics belong predominantly to the Intellectual hand type, with the sub-type of the Sociable/Artistic. I would not presume this person to be a practicing artist, but her hand gives evidence of aesthetic and cultural, and an appreciation of all things beautiful. The influence of the latter is seen in the rectangular palm, while the length of the fingers and thumb belong to the Intellectual type. The thumb and Mercury finger are of exceptional length, thus confirming a facility of expression which is inherent in both hand types.

The Sociable/Artistic type, with its element of Fire, is compatible with the element of Air, native to the Intellectual hand, because they complement each other. Fire lends life and a desire for adventure and challenge to the pure Intellectual hand, while the latter supplies the capacity for arbitration and analysis.

The thumb is of above average length and has a slender base phalange, which reveals inborn tact, but judging from the degree of inclination, the thumb is not as flexible at its base, which gives a clue that this person possesses a strong and definite will of her own; the length of the thumb further enhances the staying power of the individual and indicates self-control over impulses.

In the handwriting, versatility is seen in the two varied styles of writing, showing different sides of her personality, but not in a "Dr. Jekyll and Mr. Hyde" fashion. The right-slanted writing shows all the features of extroversion; i.e., ending strokes to the right, narrow right margin and left margin decreasing, showing stronger impulses for spending money, etc. This writing reveals the influence of the Sociable/Artistic hand type, while the left-slanted script reflects her desire for privacy and self-actualization. It reveals that she is quite content in her own company. The Greek letter formations in "d"s, "e"s and "g"s, confirm an exceptional mentality coupled with cultural interests, with an inherent facility of expression both verbally and in writing.

The major lines in the palm are well-marked and clear of obstacles. The Head line reveals an above average mental prowess, seen from its unwavering length; the line is positioned diagonally across the palm, thus indicating versatility and a creative imagination, since the end of the line reaches the sphere of the Mount of Luna. The Head line also has a fork pointing to the Mount of Mercury; this is often referred to as the "lawyer's fork." Indeed, the facility of expression, keen mental perceptions coupled with a practical common sense and objectivity seen in the "Quadrangle,"-the space between the Head and Heart lines - would be excellent assets in the legal profession.

Her innate caution is seen in the base section of the thumb, which has several horizontal markings. The thumb's angle to the hand is about 45 degrees, which reflects cautiousness and conservatism in some area.

The inherent caution or reserve described above is also evidenced in the left slant of the second writing sample, which probably originated from experiences in her childhood, as is the case with most adult left-slanted writers.

The versatility in letter formations and the mixture of garland, arcade and thread connections with pointed tops of "n"s, etc., confirm versatility and a discerning intelligence.

CAREER APTITUDES

The above described abilities would be well-suited for many professional careers where keen attention to details and an ability to grasp the core of the matter would be viable assets. A career in law would be an excellent choice.

Her perceptual qualities could be applied in a specific area of research. These qualities would also lend themselves for the teaching profession.

(She is a handwriting analyst and also works in public relations.)

Figure HW 4, B-B, The Intellectual Personality

Today I shall be doing into details before we le. It seems strange to be many woolens when the is 90 degrees, but the report from Ireland ß perature at 51 degrees

this will be our fourth trip to th and I'm looking forward as much t do to my first visit. Ireland is a but perhaps I am a little prejudiced

Figure HP 4, B, The Intellectual Personality

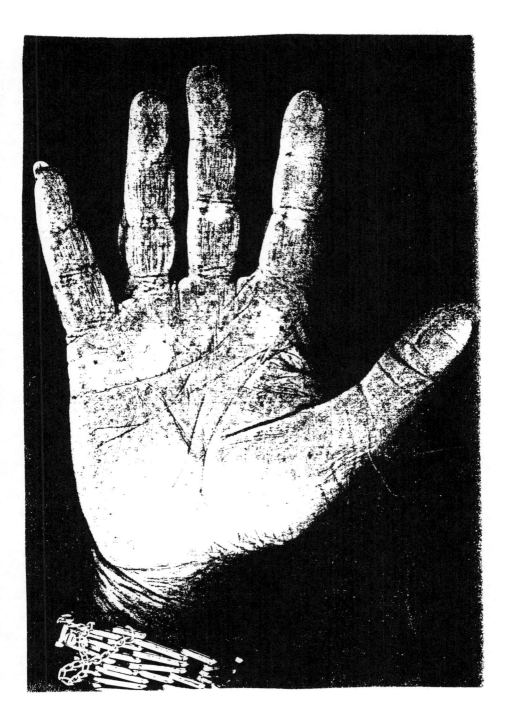

28

The Social/Artistic Personality

THIS HANDPRINT AND TWO VARIATIONS OF HANDWRITING, (HP 5 A - HW 5 A-A) belong to a female, about 50.

The hand is considered large, but since her general body build is tall and stately, her hand is therefore not out of proportion. Her primary type falls into the Sociable/Artistic category, but with a strong influence of the Intellectual type, fully described in the previous chapter. Although the rectangular palm in this sample determines its main category, the elements of Fire and Air that are native of the Sociable and Intellectual types, respectively, are both in evidence and complement each other. The presence of a very long and powerful thumb shows the influence of the Intellectual type and lends determination and perseverance to her personality; lively warmth is supplied by the Sociable type.

The skin texture of the palm is fine, but it is also firm and elastic, which brings out the best qualities of this type. It shows none of the extreme softness or flabbiness of the indulgent variety, and the well-developed mounts in the hand attest to physical and mental activities and a harmonious personality who knows how to get enjoyment out of life, evidenced primarily in the well-padded Mount of Venus and the clear, well-marked Life line.

Her sociable disposition is reflected in the rhythmic styles of both writing samples, although the first reflects the more outgoing personality of the two, indicating all the characteristics of the extrovert; i.e., right slant, ending strokes to the right, large writing, narrow right margin. The Figure 8 "g" made in "Hamburger" points to her skilful adaptability, which has been a tremendous asset to her husband's career as a World Bank official. They have lived in many different countries, where she has adjusted extremely well in all types of situations.

She mentioned that she always uses the first handwriting for notes and letters, but couldn't explain or give a reason for it. The second style of writing is meant for her personal diary or notes to herself, which shows different ways of functioning. The writing destined for others to see is larger and right-slanted, which indicates that she likes to project herself to the world as very outgoing. Her "private" writing conveys a more independent, self-sufficient person who does not need constant companionship and will be just as happy with her books and crafts, etc. Both writing styles reveal excellent word and line spacing, which attest to her intelligence and organizational skills.

The major lines engraved on the palmar surface are well-marked and positioned. The Heart line rising from between the fingers of Jupiter and Saturn reveals loyalty and dependability in her affections, while the long and gently sloping Head line, a characteristic of the Sociable/Artistic type, mirrors her creativity and resourcefulness. This is further reflected in the rounded "percussion" which is the outer edge of the hand, and the well-developed Mount of Luna, the seat of our imagination. The unusually long line of Apollo, starting from within the Mount of Venus, traverses the palm toward the Mount of Apollo. This is often referred to as the "line of success" or "brilliance," but it is foremost a sign of a happy and well-adjusted nature who possesses the ability to adjust to circumstances, even in the face of adversity. Her life so far has been a confirmation, since she has lived among many different cultures due to her husband's career. To quote her: "There has not been a place I didn't like," and she added, "more or less."

The above is also reflected in the two styles of writing which express considerable versatility. Her strong individuality is confirmed in the signature, revealing different facets of her personality. The inflexible first stroke of the signature gives evidence of her firm convictions and opinions, which she readily confirmed when I mentioned it to her, and the last encircling cover stroke reveals that while she is open and direct about most things, she does not care to divulge information about personal matters. The underscore beneath the signature reaffirms her own importance or social standing, and the rising signature mirrors her enthusiasm and optimism.

CAREER APTITUDES

The above described qualities would lend themselves well to such careers as public relations, conference planning, etc., for she is well-organized and has the ability to communicate and to influence others using the art of "gentle persuasion." These also could be attributes in careers that involve sales. Unsuitable careers would be those requiring too much routine work, that would not stimulate or challenge her sufficiently.

(She is a British homemaker with many interests in sports and arts/crafts, etc.)

Figure HW 5, A-A, The Sociable/Artistic Personality

I had lunch with Liz
went to Hamburger Ha
lunch was very goo

M. Brimble

Weekend market at
the Sanam Luang

Erawan Falls or
Elephant Falls - 67 km
north of Kanchanaburi

Figure HP 5, A, The Sociable/Artistic Personality

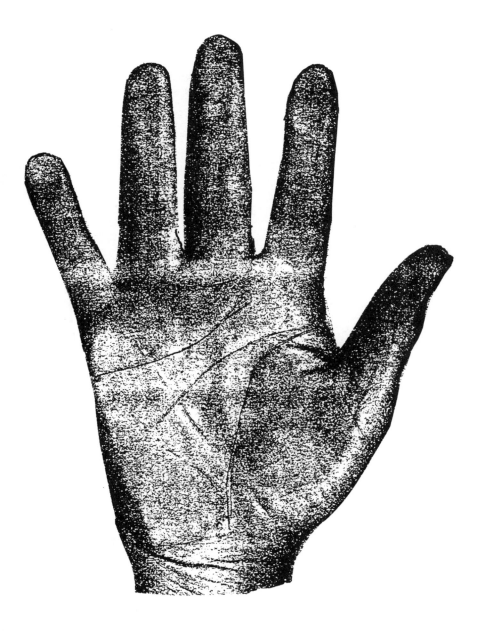

29

The Psychic/Intuitive Personality

General Characteristics:

THIS HAND IS CHIROGNOMICALLY EASILY RECOGNIZED BY A LONG, NARROW PALM and fingers. The skin texture is generally fine and flexible, and the hand is the most elegant and beautiful of all the types, especially the woman's, with its long, tapering and smooth fingers without pronounced joints.

Beside the major lines, which should be clearly visible, the palmar surface is usually covered by a network of fine lines, giving evidence to the sensitivity of the central nervous system. The Head line curves toward the Mount of Luna, revealing the imagination inherent of this hand type, which corresponds to the elements of "Water." Water is fluid and restful if contained, but is continually seeking to escape its boundaries. This element is often seen as destructive, but this is caused by the other elements, such as a wind storm or tidal wave pitching up high waves. This duality is also mirrored in the personality, as individuals of this hand type are calm on the surface, but emotional and impressionable on the inside. They are very much affected by the environment they live in; calm and peaceful surroundings will produce stability and harmony. Such people may not survive emotionally in a poor atmosphere for they have none of the robust, feisty qualities of the Practical, or the ability for rationalization of the Intellectual type. Individuals of the Psychic/Intuitive type are the least practically oriented because they are attuned to their feelings more than to their thinking. They might use phrases such as "I feel that this is the right thing to do," rather than "I think."

Due to highly developed intuition and imagination, such people often escape into a fantasy-world, and are therefore excellently suited for the acting profession. It would be natural for them to impersonate another role or to fit into various situations.

The following samples of hands and handwritings belong to a male, and a mother and daughter, whose main hand types are reflective of the Psychic/Intuitive.

THE ANALYTICAL/THEORETICAL PERSONALITY

This handprint and writing (HP 6 A - HW 6 A-A) belong to a male, about 53.

The hand is characterized by a long, rectangular palm with long fingers and a very slender thumb, which chirognomically belongs to the Psychic/Intuitive, with an influence of the Intellectual/Philosophic hand type. The element of the former is "Water," while that of the latter is "Air." This combination of the "thinking" and "feeling" types is not always compatible with practical living.

By his own admission, his former training in a technically-oriented profession, where he was called on to make quick, practical decisions, was not a good choice. He is the "thinker" and "master of possibilities," evidenced in the long first phalanges of his fingers, which dominate the middle and lower sections. This is especially apparent in the index finger which is short by comparison to the Apollo finger, and the second phalange of Jupiter is disproportionally short compared to the top and third sections, which indicates that he does not wish to be an executive, or carry the burden of responsibility for others. This is also seen in the slender thumb, which, although of good length, conveys the "theoretician" rather than the "inveterate doer."

In the handwriting, these theoretical/analytical qualities are confirmed in his connected, simplified script with pointed tops of "m"s and "n"s, giving a clue to his keen and probing mentality. The word and line spacing is wide and shows objectivity, but it also suggests a reluctance to make decisions or move toward the future; that is further reflected in the wide right margin of the writing.

The variations in the ending strokes of letters are a point of interest and reveal the duality in his personality. While some of them complete the movement to the right, indicating a rational follow-through and the desire for communication, other endings rise high in the air or even turn left-ward, which express a strong propensity toward the spiritual. These two different modes of "thinking" versus "feeling" are not always fully compatible in his nature, which is confirmed by his deliberately controlled writing, interspersed with "stunted" or retraced letters, such as in "shall," "g"s and "y"s, etc.

The major lines of Heart, Head and Life are clearly visible. The Heart line shows loyalty in the affections, while the Head line indicates a greater than average mental capacity; this line starts out straight and then curves quite rapidly toward the Mount of Luna. This suggests that in the early years his career followed a practical path, while later on it moved toward his inborn leanings toward self-expression in the arts. This is also visible in the many lines beneath the Apollo finger, which suggest various interests of a creative nature started later in his life. The long finger of Apollo confirms his artistic inclinations.

Beside the major lines, there are a host of small lines traversing the palmar surface, which reflect the sensitivity of the Psychic hand. From the horizontal lines crossing the Mount of Venus, it is apparent that this man's life has included many struggles and conflicts; fortunately, the Life line continues with greater energy and vitality in the second half of its path.

The presence of these multiple spiderweb lines also suggest a fine skin texture, which reveals the sensitivity of a "thin-skinned" disposition that has a limit of tolerance for frustration.

Sensitivity is seen in the handwriting in some of the looped "d" stems, and in the fluctuation of height and width in middle zone letters. Loyalty and high integrity are evidenced in his clearly legible script.

CAREER APTITUDES

There are many areas where these talents and qualities could be fully utilized, such as in the teaching profession where his patience with details and people, objectivity and tolerance would be excellent attributes.

Another field would be the performing arts, less as an actor than in areas where his ability to visualize would be an excellent asset, such as in directing or setting up "stage props."
The careers unsuitable are those where a person would be expected to make quick decisions in mundane, every day matters.

(This man was a former Radio Communication Technician. He now is a member of a performing dance group.)

Figure HW 6, A-A, The Analytical/Theoretical Personality

Figure HP 6, A The Analytical/Theoretical Personality

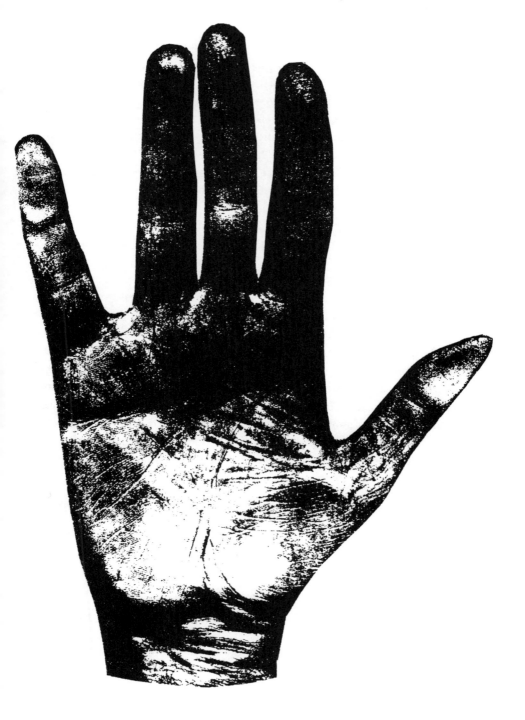

THE INTUITIVE/PRACTICAL PERSONALITY

The handprints and handwritings are those of a young mother, 33, and her daughter, age 11, (HP 6 B & C - HW 6 B-B & C-C).

The similarity in the shape of their hands and palms are remarkable, but there are dissimilarities as well, which I will discuss as they arise. The rectangular palms with smooth, tapering fingers reflect primarily the Psychic/Intuitive type, but with a strong influence of the Practical/Useful, thus combining the elements of "Water" and "Earth." Although the fingers appear long, they are only of average length, and slightly shorter in the daughter's hand; this indicates that while both are excellent with details, they are not "bogged down" by them either. The fingertips in the mother's hands are more rounded than tapered, which shows her sociable disposition. Although the thumb is slender, it is not extremely thin, which reveals a greater amount of determination and staying power than the extreme shape would indicate. Her index finger is short by comparison to the Apollo finger, giving evidence that she is not a "take-charge-type" of person; at the same time, her firm thumb shows that she can be assertive if necessary.

The daughter's hand reveals a very interesting combination of the Intuitive and the Practical types. As stated above, the shape of the palm determines its main category, but the fingers show a great variation in shapes and fingertips. The most noticeable is the Saturn finger, which seems completely out of proportion with the rest of her hand and the other fingers. By itself this would denote a strong, practical, business sense. When I pointed this out to the mother, she immediately confirmed her daughter's interest in business affairs. The daughter's index finger is the most tapered of the fingertips, revealing quick perceptions, which would complement the Saturn finger if applied to business or law, etc. Her fingers are shorter than her mother's by comparison to her own palm, which indicates the ability to act upon matters quickly, being able to make fast decisions based on practical deductions. The thumb is similar in shape to her mother's but slightly fuller, as is the lower part of the palm, which shows a desire for physical activity.

The mother's handwriting is an unhurried pattern of up and downstrokes, with most of the final movements extended to the right. This is an expression of her generosity and interest in people and the world-at-large. The presence of garland lead-in strokes to first letters reflects her adaptability and her desire to please others. Some of the lower-zone loops do not return to the base line, which indicates that she is selective in close relationships, and that she has the tendency to suppress feelings of anger or criticism that might hurt her or others by voicing them, because peace and harmony are very important to her. The dream-like quality ascribed to the Psychic/Intuitive type is seen in the capital "T" in "Tower," where the bar does not meet the stem of the letter.

The presence of different "t"-bars suggests versatility and her willingness to give in and to compromise, while the highly crossed "t"s show that where she feels strongly, she will stand up for her rights.

With regard to the daughter, it is normal that her writing should conform to the method that she was taught, yet there are certain points of interest worth mentioning. Some of the "r"s are broad, which indicates an inborn visual sense and the ability to work with her hands; she would do well in needlework or painting, and be adept at handling tools or gadgets. While some of her "m"s and "n"s are still rounded on top, as taught in the standard alphabet, some of these letters have pointed tops, which promises a keen and analytical mind.

On the palmar surface, both the mother's and daughter's major lines are clearly visible, which reveals an even-tempered disposition; the palms are not covered with a multitude of fine lines, at least not at this time. The Heart lines of both individuals are forked, but positioned differently. In the mother's hand, the branch ends on the base of the Mount of Jupiter, which reveals a very feminine nature, while the fork in the daughter's Heart line veers toward the Head line, indicating that she may have to make choices involving her emotions and a career. There is also a difference in the position and shape of the Head lines; the mother's line curves toward the Mount of Luna at a greater angle, which is inherent of the Psychic/Intuitive type, while the daughter's lies in a straight line diagonally across the palm, revealing the influence of the Practical type. Both of the lines reflect excellent concentration, seen in the clearly marked paths which are free of obstacles.

The Life lines in both hands form a wide circle around the Mount of Venus, which indicates a spirit of adventure and the desire to live a full life, but, judging from the firm thumbs, giving evidence to a certain amount of conservatism, dependability and self-control, it is unlikely that neither mother or daughter would go to extremes in any venture or ideas.

Control is seen in the mother's handwriting in the fairly even base line, although it reveals a tendency toward minor mood swings, revealed in the slight waviness of the line. Her sensitivity is further indicated in some of the looped "d" stems. The daughter's sample is written on lined paper, but it shows excellent control, since every letter is formed well and unhurriedly, confirming her dependability in her school work and at home. Her hand and handwriting both show excellent potential.

The desire to lead a full life and for physical and material gratification is expressed in the mother's and daughter's handwritings in the full lower zonal loops, and optimism is revealed in the former's rising base line.

CAREER APTITUDES

The Mother: Her abilities would lend themselves well to a position as an Administrative Assistant, where her excellent attention to details and her congenial, adaptable personality would be a great asset. She would be better suited for a smaller office, since she does not like crowds or commotion. Contrary to the Psychic/Intuitive type, due to the influence of the Practical type, she could work well with facts and figures, as in accounting, etc. Her patience, tolerance and objectivity would also be suitable in the teaching profession, especially dealing with children or handicapped people.

The Daughter: The daughter's needs and qualifications are similar in some areas, but different in others. As already mentioned, due to the greater influence of the Practical/Useful hand type, she could choose a career in business. From the potential seen in her hand, she may also be suitable for a career in law, real estate, etc.

Figure HW, 6, B-B, The Psychic/Intuitive Personality (Mother, Age 32)

The type of project y is up to you. You may experiment, observe and, a process, do a demon of a scientific principle, something, or present a la stells, rocks butterfl and talk about that.

Renee

Figure HW, 6, C-C, The Psychic/Intuitive Personality (Daughter, Age 11)

Betsy Byar's sharp perce
and skill at penetrating the
life of children have made he
of america's most popular an
writers for young people.

Stephanie Kovaloy
12/4/58

Figure HP, 6, B, The Psychic/Intuitive Personality (Mother, Age 32)

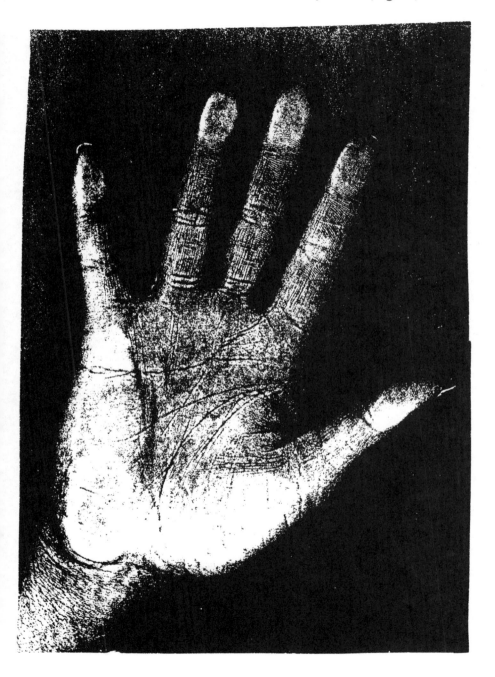

Figure HP, 6, C, The Psychic/Intuitive Personality (Daughter, Age 11)

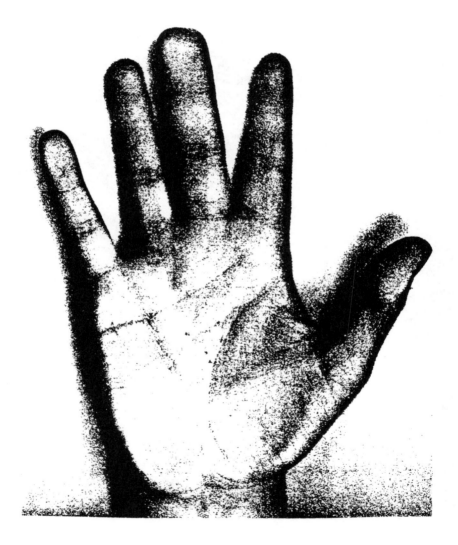

30

The Ideal Teacher

THIS HANDPRINT AND WRITING BELONG TO A FEMALE, 50, WHO IS IN THE TEACHing profession. (HP 7 A - HW 7 A-A).

The medium-sized hand bears most of its characteristics from the Intellectual category, but with the influence of the Social/Artistic and the Practical types, depicting a well-rounded personality. It seems that the right kind of ingredients are incorporated to provide an ideal profile for her chosen profession, of which she has never tired.

The fingers with rounded tips are set on a slightly rectangular palm that is rounded at the base of the fingers, showing the influence of the Social/Artistic type, while her long, slender thumb reveals tact and cultural interests. The firmness in the finger and thumb settings lends a strong determination to a sociable and gentle facade, and the length of the Jupiter finger indicates that this person welcomes responsibility in her domain.

Her handwriting confirms these findings. Its primary connective strokes are garlands mixed with arcades, and the final ending movements to the right reveal her interest in people, but her vertical slant and the regularity in the word and line spacing, as well as in the letter formations, indicate poise and self-control. The tops of "m"s and "n"s are pointed, which express her probing and keen mind.

From the linear pattern engraved on the palm, it is evident that this writer had to overcome obstacles in her early years, which is shown in the chained formation of the Heart line, and in the horizontal rays that cross the Mount of Venus. This person did not claim her parental independence at an early age, seen in the twisted joint path of the Head and Life lines, but they continue strongly after the separation, indicating that overcoming adversities made them her strength. The Head line lies diagonally across the palm with a slight bend toward the Mount of Luna, the seat of imagination and creativity. The space between the Heart and Head lines, the "Quadrangle," is wide, which reflects her tolerance and objectivity.

The presence of two Fate lines in her palm indicates her adaptability in the face of adversities. The first Fate line starts from the wrist but ends at the Head line, while the second line, starting from the Mount of Luna, traverses the palm toward the Mount of Saturn with a branch toward Jupiter. The latter indicates efforts in career and learning.

An additional marking is the "Intuition Crescent," the influence of the Psychic/Intuitive hand type, (PART II - Chapter 2) which is marked in the strong crease formation around the Mount of Luna; this reveals insight into her own personality and that of others.

Her handwriting shows a controlled yet individual rhythm that reflects balance, harmony and resilience; her calmness makes her capable of lending strong moral support to others through her own strength. The carefully formed letters in the steady unhurried writing gives a clue to her excellent attention to details and her infinite patience. The word and line spacing confirm her organizational skills and clear thinking for small and larger issues. The rounded letters in the middle zone attest to her congenial temperament, and from the zonal balance - the upper, middle and lower zone,-it is evident that she has the ability to realize her goals. This is further confirmed by the return of lower-zone loops to the base line.

THE TEACHER'S PROFILE

This person's natural and developed qualities form a cluster of characteristics excellently suited to the teaching profession:

1. Patience with subject matter and people;
2. A calm disposition;
3. Tolerance and fairness; i.e., objectivity;
4. A non-aggressive, yet firm and consistent behavior;
5. The willingness to accept responsibility (seen in long Jupiter finger);
6. Good balance between firmness and flexibility;
7. Genuine interest in helping people to help themselves.

Figure HW, 7, A-A, The Ideal Teacher

At a very young age, I knew I wante to be a teacher, and throughout my adul life I have taught, either full-time part-time, depending on the demands my family at the time, the following subjects and/or grades: nursery school first grade, adult education (English - math), English to Home-Bound Stude and, at the present time, High Scho English Composition. Also, during my summer vacations, I am a volunteer teacher of English + math for ESOL adult students (Speakers of Other Languages). I have always been a

Figure HP, 7, A, The Ideal Teacher

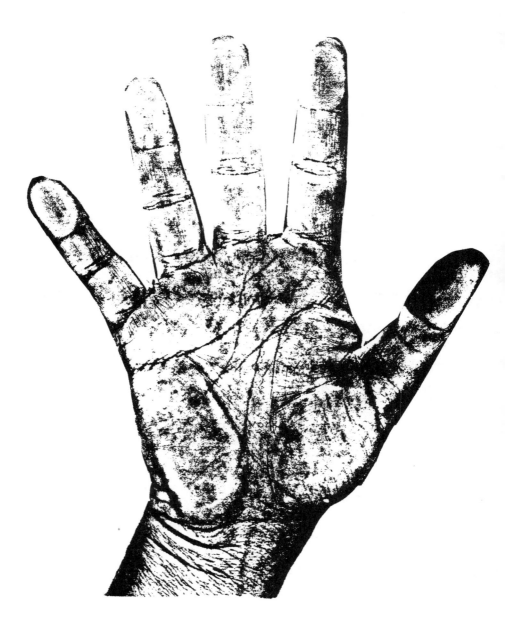

31

Gifted and Talented Personalities

THIS HANDPRINT AND WRITING BELONG TO A YOUNG FEMALE, 18, COLLEGE STUdent. (HP 8 A - HW 8 A-A).

The hand is medium to large with a slightly rectangular palm and very long fingers and extremely long thumb. Like the previous handprint of the ideal teacher, this hand is also a combination of the Intellectual/Analytical and Conic/Artistic types, yet by virtue of its unlike proportions of fingers, thumb and palm, the personality is quite different, which is especially evident from the palmar surface.

What is immediately noticeable from the handprint is the nearly 90 degree angle formed by the spread of the extremely long and slender thumb and the widely separated fingers as well. This shows an adventurous, even daring attitude. This young lady is not only enormously gifted musically, she also scored a perfect "1600 points" on the SAT's (Standard American Testing), which is impossible to beat, since it is the highest possible score.

The handwriting does not do justice to the potential seen in the hand because she is still "unfocused" at this time, but there are indications of an unusual mental capacity; i.e., the simplification in letter formations and the omission of lead-in strokes, which reveals her independence of thought and action; combining "i"-dots with the following letter, indicating resourcefulness and/or

257

ingenuity, and Greek letter formations in "d"s which show her cultural leanings.

The major lines in her hand are very clear and strong. The Heart line rising from between the fingers of Jupiter and Saturn expresses loyalty in the affections. The space between the Heart and Head lines, the "Quadrangle," is wide and clear, reflecting objectivity and a capacity for reasoning, which, coupled with the extremely long and slightly curved Head line, shows an unusual development of mental and creative faculties.

The Head and Life lines are widely separated at the starting point, which not only attests to independence and lack of conformity, but reveals a tendency toward impulsive moves and hasty decisions, especially if coupled with smooth and tapered fingers and "unknotted" joints.

The presence of a Fate line shows a strong sense of purpose and set goals. This line stops at the point in her palm that roughly symbolizes her present age.

The presence of an Intuition line, together with her long, tapered fingers, shows an inborn sixth sense that allows her to grasp ideas instinctively as well as logically.

The handwriting reflects her quick mind, and also her impulses; the latter is evidenced in the irregularity and fluctuation of letter formations, change of slant and spacing, while the versatility of her personality is revealed in the mixture of the connections; i.e., garlands, arcades and pointed tops of "n"s and "m"s. Her intuition is indicated in her primarily disconnected style of writing.

With regard to a future career, there are no limitations as to her choices because she has the kind of intelligence that allows her to do anything she wants to undertake. An unsuitable career would be one where she wouldn't be constantly challenged to explore new avenues. The disadvantage of such a characteristic, if one can call it that, is that by virtue of having too many choices, it may be hard to stick to one profession.

I wonder what Leonardo da Vinci's hands looked like, for he, the most famous Renaissance man of all times, was dissatisfied with his achievements because he focused his attention on a subject just long enough to master it, and then went on to find new challenges.

It will be interesting to follow the development of this promising young woman with regard to career and personality.

Figure HW 8, A-A, The Gifted Personality

I've started my internship (like the stationery?) and am having fun. On my first day I opened a death-threat. Neat, huh. I'm doing mostly data entry & dull stuff for my first week, but it's great. Take care,

Love Anne!

Figure HP, 8, A, The Gifted Personality

THE EXCEPTIONAL PERSONALITY

This handprint and handwriting belong to a woman of about 60, (HP 8 B - HW 8 B-B).

The hand is, at first glance, quite odd-looking. The shape of the palm is reminiscent of the Practical, or even the Elementary/Primitive type by virtue of a large, square palm with very short fingers, but the opposing exceptional feature is the powerful and extremely long thumb set low in the hand. Like the previous sample, this reveals musical talent. Another contradictory feature to the primary type is the long finger of Mercury, which shows excellent communication skills that enhance her musical talent. This person graduated from a prestigious college with a double major in music and English. She is still composing lyrics and is a colorful public speaker, aided and complemented by the genuine warmth of her personality. This is confirmed by the well-developed Mounts of Venus and Luna; the latter is the seat of imagination and the nucleus of the personality.

The handwriting shows primarily extroverted character traits, such as: a right-ward slant; ending strokes to the right, and a small right margin, which reflects her interest in people and the world-at-large. The word spacing exhibits large, intermittent gaps, which reveals that there are times when she feels deeply isolated. From the line spacing, it is evident that, where her emotions and intimate feelings are involved, she may lose her otherwise excellent judgment and objectivity. This is evidenced in the line spacing, where some of the lower-zone loops are slightly touching the lines below.

Inherent to the Practical and Elementary hand type, there are few lines besides the major ones of Life, Heart and Head imprinted on the palmar surface, but these are so unusual in strength and length that there can be no doubt as to this individual's powerful and exceptional personality. The positioning of the lines is of significance, because it shows a mentally and humanly integrated nature, thus combining the native force seen in the shape of the hands, fingers and thumb, with the mental capacity of a highly developed being.

The Head line lies diagonally across the palm, but terminates near the Mount of Luna, exhibiting practical and creative sources. The Life line, although started jointly with the Head line, continues strong and clear after the separation, combining family ties with individuality. The wide path of the Life line encircling the Mount of Venus suggests love of adventure and travel, since the line veers toward the Mount of Luna. The Life line itself expresses uninterrupted vitality and energy.

The dual forces in her personality, i.e., her inborn warmth, love of home, stability and sensuality, coupled with sophistication and mental development, is also reflected in her handwriting. Independence and abstract reasoning powers are seen in the many simplified letter formations (PART III - Chapter 2), and the omission of lead-in strokes to capital and lowercase letters are interspersed with very long "prop" or support strokes. This reveals dependence on family, traditions, etc.

The spirit of adventure is expressed by the wide expansion in the writing movement and the small right margin. The different facets and opposing forces in her personality are further reflected in the "t"-bars. While some of them are crossed high, showing a person who welcomes responsibility and loves to be in charge of things, other "t"s crossed low on the stem express the opposite, i.e., that in some area of her life she would like to be nurtured and taken care of.

CAREER APTITUDES

A person with these dynamic qualifications and charismatic personality would make a natural leader and promoter. These inborn traits cannot be taught in schools; they would also be excellent attributes in politics or as a performer.

Figure HP, 8, B, The Exceptional Personality (Shown Sideways)

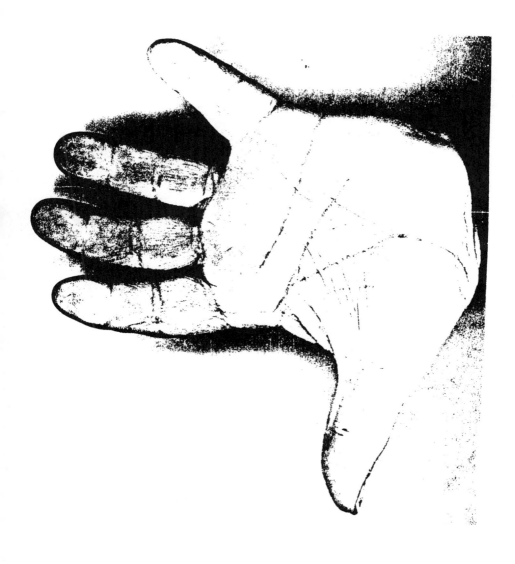

Figure HW 8, B-B, The Exceptional Personality

Dear Liz,

Am sending you the cr
you asked for. We misse
on tuesday but had a very
day - Went to the Indian C
Center (museum ground to the 12
in the area) They had crafts, -
jewelry and dancing and food
to the Zoo for a few hours.
impressive Had dinner at
and home to pack. Wednesday
for home. Millie said she w
for 2 days. I continued to tr
catch up with all I missed

Really enjoyed team
with you. You are quite
doer and have many fasci
hobbies. Let me hear

Much lov
Georgie

32

The Dynamic Communicator and the Go-Getter Personality

THE DYNAMIC COMMUNICATOR

THIS HANDPRINT AND HANDWRITING BELONG TO A FEMALE, ABOUT 50, REGIONAL Manager and very successful sales representative (HP 9 A - HW 9 A-A).

This small-sized hand is a combination of the Intellectual/Philosophic and the Psychic/Intuitive types. The handprint is distinguished from the others because of the combination of a small, square palm and the extremely long, tapered fingers, which are the influence of the Psychic/Intuitive category.

Although this person is right-handed, I am showing the left handprint, since the right print did not reveal the entire thumb, which, in this case, is an exceptional feature with regard to its length and strength, expressing the persistence and staying power of this individual.

The unusual constellation in the hand is seen in the thumb, very long and strong Jupiter, and dominating first phalange of the Mercury finger, (PART I, Chapters 3 and 4). The unusually long Jupiter finger reveals this person's quest for leadership, which she has attained in great measure. Long fingers also indicate patience and keen attention to details, while the squareness of the palm exhibits a desire to deal with large issues, and for finding viable solutions to problems.

The slender and long Mercury finger with its dominant top phalange indicates her powers of persuasion; these are inborn character-

istics that have contributed to her success, first as a top sales representative, then as a regional manager. Since she also possesses the
congeniality and adaptability of the Psychic/Intuitive type, she is adept
in handling business and personal relationships.

The handwriting reflects many of the characteristics stated
above. The right slant and extending final strokes, as well as the
small right margin, confirm interest in people and world-directedness, while the rising lines give evidence of her ambition and/
or enthusiasm. This is further revealed in some of the "t"-bars
placed high on the stem. The clearly legible yet moderately fast
writing shows her attention to details, seen in some of the "i"s
dotted directly over the letter, while others, placed high, express
her perception of ideas and situations.

The word and line spacing reveals organizational skills; the
words are not separated widely which is the mark of a natural
leader, for spontaneous, natural expression does not allow for
very wide distances. From the line spacing, it is evident that she
is capable of dealing with large issues as well.

The major lines in her left and right hand are very similar. There
is good spacial and zonal balance between the Heart and Head lines,
referred to as the "Quadrangle;" this indicates tolerance and clear
reasoning. The Head line curves toward the Mount of Luna, revealing
the influence of the Psychic/Intuitive category. The presence of an
"Intuition Crescent," (PART II - Chapter 8), encircling the Mount of
Luna, discloses an innate sixth sense that lets her grasp opportunities
instinctively as well as logically. The Head and Life lines are separated from each other at their inception by a narrow margin, which
shows potential leadership, because such a person is not bound to
conservative ideas as much as individuals in whose hands these two
lines are joined at the starting point. This separation of lines also
reveals independence of ideas and daring, but without letting the impulse take over which is suggested by a wide division.

The above is reflected in the handwriting in the bold use of
space, the rising lines and highly crossed "t"-bars, and last but
not least, in her signature.

THE PROFILE OF THE DYNAMIC COMMUNICATOR

Seen from the Hand:
1. Practical common sense, exhibited in the square palm;
2. Long, slender fingers and thumb, which let her grasp opportunities quickly;
3. Staying power and endurance, seen in the powerful and very long thumb;
4. Inborn sixth sense, indicated in the "Intuition Crescent" and tapering fingertips;
5. Leadership potential and desire for responsibility, revealed in the very long finger of Jupiter;
6. Communication skills, and the gift to influence others, expressed in the long finger of Mercury and its top phalange.

Seen in the Handwriting:
7. World-directedness and interest in people, seen in the right slant;
8. World-directedness and interest in people, seen in ending strokes to right;
9. World-directedness and interest in people, seen in small right margin;
10. Optimism and ambitious drive, seen in rising lines and "t"-bars;
11. Versatility, seen in mixture of garlands, arcades, thread and angles.

Figure HP, 9, A, The Dynamic Communicator (Left Hand)

Figure HW, 9 A-A, The Dynamic Communicator

There's about 5 couples we see fr (outside of the club) + mostly previous Maryland! We spent a lovely Sede of their homes.

Mazel tov to Jerry + Natalie - great news. I know you must enjoying your granddaughters. I', for grandchildren to play with, afraid I'll have to wait.

Howard is fine + doing well & Sully is getting started in his 'ne Stocks, insurance - he got his bro. license.

Hope you and Norm are both will pay us a visit!

Much love + regards both of us -

Barb

THE GO-GETTER PERSONALITY

This handprint and writing belong to a young man, 21, left-handed, college student. (HP 9 B - HW 9 B-B).

The broad hand is almost perfectly square, and its main type falls into the Practical/Useful category, with the sub-type of the Social/ Artistic, indicated in the tapered, slender fingertips. The fingers are short by comparison to the length of the palm, but not stubby or clumsy, and the fingertips are of varied shapes. The Jupiter finger is the most tapered, indicating quickness in perceptions. The length of the Mercury finger, with the top section dominating the other two, reveals communication skills and the ability to influence others. The Mercury finger is also called the "finger of enterprise and/or business" if it belongs to the Square hand; if on the Intellectual, it may enhance the scientific area, and if on a musician's, it confirms musical talent.

The firm but thick palm with its strong development of the lower, physical/instinctual side, indicates a vast reservoir of physical energy, which, if harnessed into creative and constructive endeavors, can be a positive force. Such a person has an absolute need of physical activity, and he should choose a profession or outside interests that would allow the use of both mental and physical energies. Resourcefulness is indicated in the rounded "percussion," the outer edge of the palm, which enhances the above characteristics when they are properly channeled. The well-developed Mounts of Upper and Lower Mars, (PART I - Chapter 6), reveal a "fighting spirit" that does not give up easily.

In the handwriting, many of the above mentioned characteristics are confirmed. The rising lines and forceful, dynamic "t"-bars, right slanted writing in spite of being left-handed, the small right margin and the heavy pressure, all attest to the energetic driving force, which is my reason for calling this the "go-getter personality." The hooks at "t"-bars suggest an appreciation of materialistic values, and sharp upstrokes or lead-in strokes in some letters further reflect impatience in getting where he wants to go, confirming the fighting spirit evidenced in the hand.

The lines imprinted on the palmar surface are unusual in the Square hand, since this type generally comes equipped with few lines beside those of Life, Head and Heart. The presence of a forked Head line, with a branch toward the center of the palm suggests that this young man is able to see "both sides of a coin," which works to his advantage, since it balances the inherent inflexibility of this hand type. The Head line itself is powerful in length and marking, terminating on the Mount of Luna, the sphere of creative imagination.

The presence of a Fate line in the Square hand is of much greater significance than if found on the Psychic/Intuitive or Social/Artistic. It adds another dimension to the Practical/Materialistic personality by mixing the elements of "Fire" with the "Earth" qualities. Although this creates a complexity in the personality, it can work favorably if well-directed.

The handwriting reflects this young man's strong drive, and independence is shown by the omission of most lead-in strokes in his abstract, simplified writing style with predominantly angular connections. Analytical qualities are also indicated in pointed tops of "m"s and "n"s, and his ambitious, optimistic drive is reflected in the rising lines.

The "Dynamic Communicator" and the "Go-Getter" have many characteristics in common, and are dissimilar in others. The latter are marked with an asterisk.

Seen in the Hand:
1. Practical business sense, seen in the square shape of the palm;
* 2. Desire for quick actions and results;
3. Strong will and endurance is seen in the forceful thumb;
4. Quick perceptions, seen in tapered fingertips of Mercury and Jupiter;
5. Long first phalange of Mercury finger enhances business sense and the ability to influence others;
* 6. Highly developed Mounts of Venus and Luna; absolute need of physical activity; energy.

Seen in the Handwriting:
7. World-directedness, interests in people and/or projects, seen in right slant;

8. The same characteristics seen in ending strokes to the right;
9. The same characteristics seen in small right margin;
10. Optimism and ambitious drive, seen in rising lines and "t"-bars;
* 11. Impatience about getting things started and/or finished, seen in sharp "tics" on upstrokes and "t"-bars and angular connectives.

CAREER APTITUDES

His qualities would be well-suited for a business-managerial position, where his ability to make quick, rational decisions would be an asset. His leadership potential and desire to combine mental and physical energies could also be applied in careers such as the Armed Forces.

Unsuitable professions: where too much routine work or attention to minor details would be expected.

Figure HW 9, B-B, The Go-Getter Personality

Dear Sir,
I regret to inform
that your presence w/ou
as the executive adminju
soon be terminated. We
be however keeping yu
the holiday season. The
plan which you are on

Figure HP, 9, B, The Go-Getter Personality

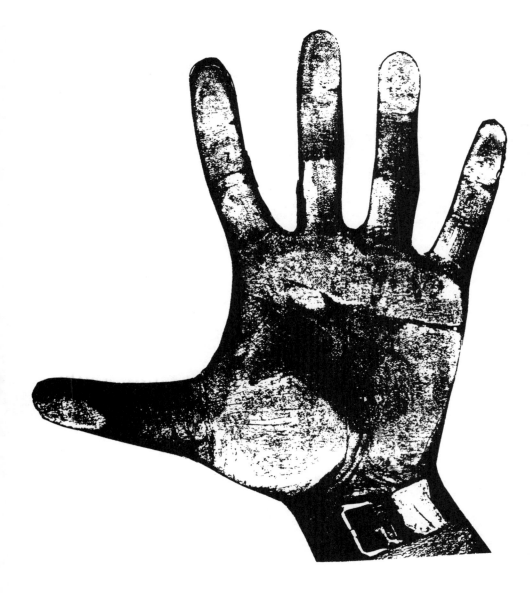

Glossary

PALMISTRY

Apollo   Finger: Ring finger. Symbolizes Beauty and the Arts. Also stands for intimate commitments; bearer of wedding ring. Line: Line below Ring finger; enhances the above qualities. Mount: Elevation below Apollo finger also enhances these traits.

Bracelets   Lines at the wrist. There are usually three in number. If well-defined, they suggest good health.

Cheiro   19th Century famous palmist, author and lecturer.

Fate Line   Also called "Line of Destiny" or Effort Line." Usually found in the center of the palm. Not a major line and is not found in all hands. Indicates goal orientation and adaptability.

Girdle of Venus   Seen below the Index, Middle and Ring fingers. Not seen in all hands. Indicates sensitivity and desire for romance.

Head Line   Also called the Line of Mentality. It is a Major line and indicates mental capacity and concentration.

Heart Line   This is a Major line and indicates the quality of this organ. The direction of the line gives a clue to our affections.

Intuition Crescent   A semi-circular line found at the edge of the hand in the lower part of the palm; shows intuition and often a sixth sense.

Jupiter   Finger: This is the index finger and relates to leadership ability and responsibilities. Mount: Elevation below this finger. If well-developed, it enhances these qualities.

Life Line   This is a Major line and is considered the most important one. Runs in a semi-circular path around the thumb.

Luna, Mount   This is an elevation in the lower part of the palm, showing creative imagination, if well-developed.

Marriage Lines   Horizontal lines below the little finger. Also called "Relationship Lines." The desire to enter intimate relationships and commitments.

Mars Mounts   There are two mounts, i.e. Upper Mars, seen at the insertion of the thumb, symbolizes a fighting spirit if well-developed. Lower Mars is at the edge of the hand below the little finger and if well-padded, it shows endurance and persistence.

Mercury Finger: This is the little finger and symbolizes the art of communication in all fields; also called the "finger of enterprise". Mount: The elevation below this finger. If well-developed, it enhances these qualities.

Mystic Cross This is a cross found in the center of the palm between the lines of Head and Heart. Shows an interest in mysticism and occult.

Percussion This is the outer edge of the palm. If rounded, it is a sign of resourcefulness and ingenuity.

Phalanges This is the name for the three sections in fingers and thumb, i.e., nail phalange, middle and base phalange.

Saturn Finger: Middle finger. It symbolizes home, stability and fairness. Mount: Elevation below this finger. Well developed enhances these qualities. Flat mount shows disappointment.

Symian Line The fusion of the two major lines of Head and Heart.

Venus Mount The root of the thumb. If well-developed, it enhances vitality and a desire for love and affections.

Writer's Fork A split Head line indicating an inclination for writing.

GRAPHOLOGY

Angle Angular form of connecting letters; symbolizes an aggressive personality and determination.

Arcade A connecting stroke in the form of an arcade. Can symbolize caution and introversion, but is also form of creativity.

Base Line The bottom of the lowercase letters. Symbolizes the ground we walk on.

Congruent If text of writing and signature are similar in style and size. Indicates courage of conviction and honesty, if legible.

Copy-book Writing The writing of an adult who adheres strictly to the method taught in school. Lack of individuality. Conformity.

Garland Form of connection in rhythmic movement, open on top of small-case letters. Symbolizes receptive, open personality, extroversion.

Neglected Writing   Illegible, irregular writing ductus. Sows decrease of mental or physical functioning.

Original Letter Formations   It symbolizes ingenuity or individuality.

Pastose Writing   Heavy or smeary writing. Usually produced with a broad nibbed pen. Indicates lack of precision.

PPI   This is the shortened name for the Personal Pronoun I.

Print Script   Different styles of printing, i.e. "block" or all-capital printing, lower-case mixed with capital letters and mixture of the above. Usually employed for mechanical drawing, business.

Retracing   This refers to unnecessary retracing of letters, indicating either nervousness, dishonesty or manipulative behavior.

Rhythm   The individual movement of the writing. Disturbed rhythm shows mental or physical difficulties.

Slant   The degree of inclination of letters in writing i.e., right, vertical left, showing compliance, self-reliance and defiance, respectively. Mixed slant indicates indecision, unreliability.

Thread   A connecting stroke in the form of a thread. It may indicate diplomacy and quick thinking in fast writing.

Zones   Symbolizing the three zones in writing, i.e., upper zone for capital letters, t-bars. Middle zone: lower-case letters, also called the "m-zone". Lower zone: lower zone loops and letter "f", which goes through all three zone.

Zonal Balance   This is a writing in which all three zones are balanced, indicating balance and harmony in the personality of the writer.

Resource List

Amend, Karen and Ruiz, Mary S., *Handwriting Analysis, The Complete Basic Book,* Newcastle Publishing, 1980.

Brandon-Jones, David, *Practical Palmistry,* CRCS Publications, 1986.

Cheiro, *Language of the Hand,* 34th printing, ARC Books, 1868.

Cheiro, *Cheiro's Complete Palmistry,* University Books, 1968.

Daniels Squire, Elizabeth, *Fortune in Your Hands,* Fleet Publishing, 1960.

Daniels Squire, Elizabeth, *Palmistry Made Practical,* Wilshire Book Company, 1960.

Gettings, Fred, *The Book of the Hand,* The Hamlyn Publishing Company, 1965.

Gettings, Fred, *The Book of Palmistry,* Triune Books, London, 1974.

Gettings, Fred, *Palmistry Made Easy,* Wilshire Book Company, 1966.

Hearns, Rudolf S., *Handwriting, An Analysis Through its Symbolism,* Vantage Press, 1966.

Jaquin, Noel, *Scientific Palmistry,* George H. Doran Co., London.

Hipskind, *Palmistry, The Whole View,* Llewellyn Publishing, 1977.

Marcuse, Irene, *Guide to Personality,* ARCO Publishing, 1980.

Mendel, Alfred O., *Personality in Handwriting,* Stephen Day Press, 1947.

Olyanova, Nadya, *Handwriting Tells,* Bobbs Merrill Co., Inc., 1936-1969.

Olyanova, Nadya, *The Psychology of Handwriting,* Ace Books, 1978.

Peckman, Elizabeth, *Your Fortune in Your Hands,* Ace Star Books, 1968.

Roman, Klara G., *Handwriting, A Key to Personality,* Pantheon Books, 1952.

Roman, Klara G., *Encyclopedia of the Written Word,* Frederic Ungar Publishing, 1968.

Simmons, Meier, Nellie, *Lion's Paws,* Barrows, Mussey Publishing, 1937.

278

Bibliography

GRAPHOLOGY

Karen Amend and Mary S. Ruiz, *Handwriting Analysis, The Complete Basic Book,* Newcastle Publishing, 1980.

Hal Falcon, Ph.D., *How To Analyze Handwriting,* Trident Press, 1964.

Rudolf S. Hearns, *Handwriting, An Analysis Through its Symbolism,* Vantage Press, 1966.

Sheila Kurtz, *Grapho-Types,* Crown Publishers, Inc., 1963.

Irene Marcuse, *Guide to Personality,* ARCO Publishing, 1980.

Alfred O. Mendel, *Personality in Handwriting,* Stephen Day Press, 1947.

Nadya Olyanova, *Handwriting Tells,* Bobbs Merrill Co., Inc., 1936-1969.

Nadya Olyanova, *The Psychology of Handwriting,* Ace Books, 1978.

Klara G. Roman, *Handwriting, A Key to Personality,* Pantheon Books, 1952.

Klara G. Roman, *Encyclopedia of the Written Word,* Frederic Ungar Publishing, 1968.

Erich Singer, *A Manual of Graphology,* Crescent Books, 1987.

Herry O. Teltscher, *Handwriting, Revelation of Self,* Hawthorn Books, Inc., 1971.

PALMISTRY

Gerry E. Biccum, *Handology,* Beyond Words Publishing, Inc., 1989.

David Brandon-Jones, *Practical Palmistry,* CRCS Publications, 1986.

Marcel Broekman, *The Complete Encyclopedia & Practice of Pamistry,* Prentice Hall, London, U.S., 1972.

Cheiro, *Language of the Hand,* 34th printing, ARC Books, 1868.

Cheiro, *Cheiro's Complete Palmistry,* University Books, 1968.

Elizabeth DanielsSquire, *Fortune in Your Hands,* Fleet Publishing, 1960.

Elizabeth Daniels Squire, *Palmistry Made Practical,* Wilshire Book Company, 1960.

Fred Gettings, *The Books of the Hand,* The Hamlyn Publishing Company, 1965.

Fred Gettings, *The Book of Palmistry,* Triune Books, London, 1974.

Fred Gettings, *Palmistry Made Easy,* Wilshire Book Company, 1966.

Judith Hipskind, *Palmistry, The Whole View,* Llewellyn Publishing, 1977.

Noel Jaquin, *Scientific Palmistry,* George H. Doran Co., London.

Bettina Luxon with Linda Dearsley, *Your Hand in Business,* Rosters Ltd., London.

Nellie Simmons Meier, *Lion's Paws,* Barrows, Mussey Publishing, 1937.

Elizabeth Peckman, *Your Fortune in Your Hands,* Ace Star Books, 1968.

Index

Analysis by Mail

If you would like to have a professional mail analysis of your handwriting and hands done by the author, or if you have any questions regarding *Handwriting & Palmistry,* you may write to:

Liz Gerstein
P.O. Box 59233
Potomac, MD   20859-9233

Please remember to enclose a stamped, self-addressed business envelope with your query. Thank you.

Handwriting & Palmistry
may be ordered from
Publishers Distribution Service by:

Calling Toll Free
1-800-345-0096

Calling in Michigan & outside U.S.
1-616-276-5196

Fax Orders
1-616-276-5197

Mail Orders to:
Publishers Distribution Service
6893 Sullivan Road
Grawn, Michigan 49637

Visa and MasterCard accepted
Quantity discounts are available.